D0095606

Fowl to the Bone

A Sebastien Saint-Gemmes Mystery

Cedric Fichepain, CEC

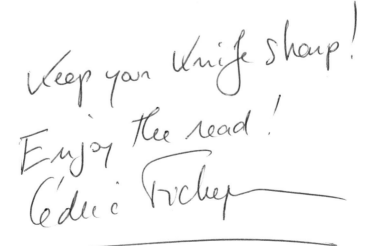

Keep your knife sharp!

Enjoy the read!

Cedric Fiche—

Copyright ©2015 Cedric Fichepain

All rights reserved under International and Pan-American Copyright Conventions. No reproduction, storage, or retrieval of this material in any media in current use or invented in the future is permissible without direct written permission from the author and/or publisher.

Because of the dynamic nature of the Internet, any web addresses or links contained in this book may have changed since publication and may no longer be valid.

This is a work of fiction. All of the characters, names, incidents, organizations, events, places and dialogue in this novel are either the products of the author's imagination or are used fictitiously.

This book is dedicated to my wife, Desarae, for her continuous support of my numerous projects.

It would also have been impossible to write this story without the help of my great staff at Le Voltaire and Le Petit Paris Bakery.

Thanks also to Robin, for inspiring me to write, and to Lisa, for keeping me on continuous deadlines and finally Rosemary D. for her fine tune proofreading.

Chapter 1

The enormous kitchen was pristine except for the dead body on the floor. A set of Messermeister knives, along with other high-end trappings, indicated this had to be the domain of a chef, or at least a very serious foodie. The size and architecture of the entire house showed it belonged to someone extremely wealthy. If the dead man was the owner, of course, none of that would help him now.

The corpse was already livid, and dark bruises around the throat punctuated the pallor. The midsection was bloated and horrendously distorted, and a thick yellow substance was crusted around the mouth. The eyes bulged, but it was impossible to tell what the sole cause of this was. The bruises around the throat were telltale signs of strangulation, so suffocation or asphyxiation was likely the cause of death. Only an autopsy could prove that conclusively.

However, it didn't take a medical examiner to determine other causes of the bulging eyes. Abject fear preceding death could make the eyes bulge too, and the monstrous method of murder here indicated that the victim's last moments on earth were filled with nothing short of terror. ...

****

As I took a sip of cold water from my white plastic cup, I was brought back to reality by the sound of a plate breaking on the floor.

"Damn it, guys, be careful!" I yelled in the direction of the culprits. Turning to another member of my staff, I shouted

"Sam, order up on table 4! Hurry up! It's been here for four minutes already, and I need the room for more plating."

"Yes, Chef," Sam responded, checking his order pad.

"Do it!" My shout was more of a scream this time, but all the while I kept working, sautéing vegetables in a hot pan.

Sometimes I wondered which of my two jobs was more stressful: chef/restaurateur or homicide detective.

It was eight o'clock on a Saturday night, and the restaurant was packed. The orders kept pouring in at lightning speed through the kitchen printer, and the noise in the kitchen was deafening.

I took a new order off the printer: Four guests. One charcuterie plate, one scotch egg and one lentil-goat app., followed by a rack of lamb, medium rare; a duck breast, medium rare; turkey leg confit and escolar, the fish special, no rice, extra veggies.

As I split the ticket, giving the yellow and white copies to my line cooks, I started shaking the pan with the vegetables, adding salt and pepper and killing the fire.

"We have a full house!" Moose boomed as he entered the kitchen. "We have a wait list of thirty minutes. Let's crank up some dinner, please, starting with table 5."

"Coming up, Moose," I said.

Moose and I met more than twenty years ago, at the Culinary Institute of Omaha, fondly known as the CIO. Although he was twenty years my senior, we became friends soon after meeting and have been very tight ever since. Moose's real name was Michael Stamelier, and he and I co-owned the Drunken Frog gastro pub, which we started ten years ago. Moose was usually in the kitchen, on the line—"driving the bus," as we called it—but tonight was my night. Every so often, he let me be in charge of the kitchen, just as I had been many years ago. That is, when my other job did not get in the way.

Tonight Moose was dressed in a nicely pressed shirt and

a bright-blue tie. It was strange to see him operating as maître d', as opposed to his usual chef mode, complete with coat and pants. I knew he enjoyed interfacing with customers, which enabled him to see first-hand how the front of the house was running so that he could correct mistakes in the kitchen. Besides being out of his domain though, Moose always looked a bit uncomfortable in dress clothes. He was a big guy: six foot four, with shoulders that would make Mike Tyson look like a ballerina. Moose had played football at the University of Nebraska–Lincoln, and he could have gone pro. Instead, he decided to go to California to cook hamburgers in a shack on the beach. He got the nickname Moose from a hunting trip in Alaska many years ago, when he'd shot and killed a huge moose. To this day, the beast was the largest moose ever recorded: a whopping 2,400 pounds of meat. To me, though, the funniest thing about Moose was his big mustache, which made him look like a porn star from the 1970s. He loved that mustache! In the twenty years I'd known him, I'd never seen him without it.

Moose watched me plating. "The mayor is in the house, Seb, Table 25," he said. "He's with your boss. Four guests, for your info," he added with smile.

"Why did they have to come here? I see them all the freaking time! There are plenty of restaurants in town." But I said it with a smile.

"Be nice, Seb," Moose said, laughing as he went back out front.

"Yeah, yeah. Okay." I laughed too. I was actually pleased to know my boss and the mayor were in the house; it meant they enjoyed our place and were spending some money.

Omaha was considered the city with the most restaurants per capita in the United States—which, by the way, was not true—and so it was often a test market for national chains. Such establishments were not exactly the best friends of independently owned restaurants like ours. It was hard to compete with them, but we had the advantage of being a local favorite, and we had many regulars. The Drunken Frog was located in the Old Market area of downtown Omaha. It held up to 120 people in the main dining room and had a private party room for 60. It also had a large full bar in a classical U shape, with all the different types of liquor imaginable, a wine list that included many *Wine Spectator* award winners, and some amazing local micro brews. The atmosphere of the restaurant was a cross between a British pub and a modern farm-to-table/"green" concept. We tried to work as much as we could with local businesses for purchasing all of our food, so the locavores were loyal to us. Nebraska, especially Omaha, offered a rich pool of suppliers and producers. We were close enough to the airport to receive daily arrivals of fresh fish and other products not available through regular local food purveyors.

More orders were printing, and as I yelled those orders in the loud, busy kitchen, I noticed that the salad, prepared by my youngest and newest employee, was overdressed and looked too soggy.

"Benjamin, you need to put less dressing on your salad. Add the dressing on the side of your mixing bowl; it will help you gauge the amount of liquid for your mixing. Now hurry! They have been waiting for their salads for awhile now."

"Yes Chef! Sorry Chef!" he said.

Benjamin was a recent graduate of the CIO, and he had a very promising future in the business. I recruited him directly from the school, and we had him start from the bottom echelon at the restaurant: peeling vegetables all day and being the "salad boy" on the line at night. This was going to be a six-month test for him, to see if he could withstand the pressure and lack of creativity that came with being a junior cook.

As I was about to read a new ticket my boss, Randy Lewis, Chief of the Omaha Police Department, popped his head through the kitchen door.

"Good evening, Detective Saint-Gemmes," he said with a smile. "You are looking very Gordon Ramsay in your chef coat tonight." When I smiled back he added, "We are having a great time! Interesting way to enjoy your Saturday night."

"Thank you for coming," I said. "Enjoy your weekend."

"See you later," he said over his shoulder as he turned left toward the restrooms.

I turned back to the orders, directing my line cooks. This Saturday night I was happy to be wielding my chef's knife, not my OPD revolver.

Chapter 2

The Handler was having dinner at one of the hippest new restaurants on the Las Vegas Strip called the Garden Bounty. It was THE new place to eat in town, with a concept based on vegetarian and vegan food. This was the latest trend for foodies, and those who followed the food-circle news. This eatery was owned in part by one of the inspiring chefs who had won on the You've Been Chopped *TV series. He impressed so many of the judges with his vegetarian and vegan dishes that they invested in him immediately, and he opened the restaurant just six months after taping the show.*

The Handler sipped a glass of Sauvignon Blanc from an organic winery in Napa Valley. He enjoyed the feeling of drinking an organic wine. That great nectar was produced with no synthetic fertilizers, pesticides, or herbicides. He appreciated the extra work that went on behind the scenes to craft wine the natural way, and he did not mind paying the extra cost. This wine was crisp and refreshing, and it felt so right in comparison to the blistering outside temperature of Vegas in late August. After sipping his wine for a while, he decided to order the tasting menu, which consisted of six courses. He was suspicious of fancy restaurants where the portions were small and did not satisfy him. On the other hand, he hated chain restaurants where the portions were out of hand and you could easily have lunch for the rest of the week with the leftovers.

He really hoped he would not be disappointed. Where he came from, overcooked meat, potatoes and canned green peas were the perennial menu. He'd soon grown sick of it. Fifteen years ago he'd decided to go vegetarian, but he still ate fish and eggs. However, he had not made the jump to vegan. He considered vegans to be nothing more than a bunch of extremists, even terrorists, who were pretty much hijacking the world of food. No food with any animal content. That did make it pretty difficult to get a balanced diet.

He stopped his musings and returned to the moment. All he cared about right now was enjoying an incredible meal. He always liked to treat himself nicely before a job.

"Here's your first appetizer sir," said the waitress, Amanda, in her cute southern accent- poached white asparagus with broccolini, pea blossoms, Manchego cheese and fire-roasted red peppers. It is served with our ten-grain sourdough bread made daily by our in-house baker."

"Thank you Amanda," he responded, smiling.

The grin on his face was not for the stunning beauty from the Deep South who'd given him her background earlier. His eyes were wide open to the first dish- it was a work of art. Different colors and textures covered the dish, which looked like a tile. The asparagus and the broccolini were blanched to perfection, and the pea blossoms were fried in a tempura batter so light and white that it looked almost surreal.

The Handler's mouth started to water. He picked up his knife and fork, and oh so slowly cut into the perfect, strategically positioned food.

"Wow! This is absolutely wonderful!" he said in a voice that was almost too loud. The tastes danced in his mouth; the flavors and scents of the red pepper and the Manchego cheese from Spain were marrying each other in an incredible way. He took a bite of his warm bread and sauced all his plate. He wanted more. ...

"It looks like you enjoyed your first course sir," Amanda said when she returned to his table. "The kitchen will be glad to see that."

"Hit me again with those bursts of flavor, please!" the

Handler responded.

"Coming right up," Amanda said with a gracious smile, turning around after picking up his plate and silverware.

He sipped through his entire glass of Sauvignon Blanc, mentally charting his plan for the rest of the evening. First, he would go to the casino and gamble for a while at the Callegio, where his target was working. The Handler knew he would have time to enjoy a great night before performing his finale.

"One-hour poached hen's egg with morel mushrooms, Swiss chard and licorice," Amanda said, introducing the new dish with such elegance that he almost fell into a trance. "It is served with a fresh brioche," she added, asking, "Would you care for another glass of wine?"

"No thank you. I have to go to work after, so I need to stay sober. Plus, I want to enjoy this amazing meal."

Amanda flashed another gracious, beautiful smile. "All right sir. Enjoy!"

The second dish was even better than the first. He could not wait for the rest, and he almost forgot the long night awaiting him.

The remaining courses of the dinner were flawless: crispy silken tofu with Georgia peaches, red curry and zucchini flowers, miso with red cabbage, turnip confit and ponzu, cantaloupe sorbet with anise shortbread and Iberian date consommé, and finally, mocha ice cream with almond dacquoise and steamed cardamom cake.

The Handler was feeling great. He was in his element tonight, with all this beauty around him. Dressed in a Hugo Boss suit, he could feel the women in the restaurant all looking at him. In his mid-forties, with dark hair lined with some gray, he displayed confidence in his movements and actions that gave him an aura of intelligence as well as beauty.

After leaving a 30 percent tip on an already huge bill, the Handler left the restaurant, taking a cab to the Callegio. He did not care too much about any costs during his stay; his employer was taking care of all that. The cab dropped him at the main entrance of the casino, and as he got out of the car his phone rang. Handing money for the fare to the cab driver, he pressed the button to receive the incoming call, not even looking at the number on the screen.

"Hello," the Handler said, knowing full well who was calling him. He started to walk toward the entrance.

"Still on target for tonight?" asked the voice.

"Yes. Everything is on schedule," the Handler replied. "The duck is warming up and will be cooked in the morning."

"We will talk again in a few days. Enjoy Vegas! It is on the house," the voice said before the line went dead.

The Handler smiled slowly as he sat at a blackjack table facing Tartufo, one of the best Italian restaurants in the nation. A few couples stood at the hostess podium waiting for tables to open. The place looked as busy as he expected it would. He still had a few hours to go before the job, and he wanted to enjoy some Vegas craziness. So as not to attract too much attention, he decided to play twenty-dollar hands. After ordering a Glenrothes single malt scotch, he once again reviewed in his head the entire plan for the rest of the evening. Patience was his stock in trade, and he knew he would need a lot of it in the upcoming week.

"Blackjack," the dealer said with a smile. "First hand, first win. Lucky night, I guess," he added in his casino customer-service voice.

"Yes, I feel confident tonight will be a great night," the Handler replied.

But in his head, the wheels were turning more in the direction of his target. His "duck," as he referred to the man, was supposed to leave for home at around two, after working all night at Tartufo.

That was when the Handler would strike.

****

Chef Bob Dewey plated his last table at 1:16 a.m.: Wagyu beef served with smoked bacon demi-glace sauce and salt-encrusted branzino. He had learned from his waiter that the guests were newlyweds, so he had decided to offer them dessert as a token of good luck. He thought he would also stop by their table to offer his personal good wishes. In general, customers loved to see the chef come out of the kitchen, and he loved to do that for the publicity and fame. He still was having so much fun working the line. He was addicted to the adrenaline and excitement of a busy kitchen. True, he couldn't enjoy it as much as he had in the past, since his knees were starting to give him trouble. But he still enjoyed working a few weekend nights every month, going from one of his restaurants to another, all across the United States. After more than forty years in the business, he owned a Latin American concept called Abajo in New York; a French restaurant, Chanterelles, in Miami; a classic California cuisine place called Eden in Napa Valley; and, of course, Tartufo in the Callegio in Las Vegas. He had plenty to keep him busy, plus many TV appearances on cable and the regular networks. He was a favorite on the cooking shows as well as the morning talk shows, and he did book tours and signings whenever he had a new cookbook out. Chef Bob Dewey was known all across the country, and he was proud of it.

He had started his career in restaurants in the same way that many chefs of the older generation had: at the bottom of the ladder, washing dishes. His start was at the Waldorf Astoria in New York when he was just fifteen. Master Chef Van Purden, the Chef de Cuisine at the Waldorf at that time, eventually took Bob under his wing. He learned all the stations in the brigade de cuisine, the kitchen system invented by renowned Chef Georges Auguste Escoffier at the beginning of the twentieth century.

Bob Dewey started as an apprentice, peeling piles of potatoes and carrots for hours on end. He never gave up, and was then promoted to commis, the equivalent of a junior cook. He worked at the Waldorf for a few years, perfecting the art of many of the different stations—legumier, friturier, grillardin, potager, etc.—and finally becoming the sous-chef at the age of twenty-two. When Van Purden died, Bob was promoted to executive chef. He was twenty-four years old.

He fell in love with Elizabeth, the daughter of an important food supplier in New York, and after a few years of dating they were married.

Bob continued his successful career throughout the United States and Europe, becoming popular when PBS started to air a cooking show on TV. There was no Food Network at that time. He then started to open a few restaurants, which he decided to manage hands-on, traveling across the country with his wife.

It was a great life.

He was done for the night. Time to drink a glass of wine and then call it a day. First, he went to his office to change. A beautiful freshly pressed chef coat was waiting for him, complete with the Tartufo logo, his name and the title of executive chef. He put on the coat but decided to leave the hat on the desk. He then went to the wine cellar and decided on a 2006 Ladera Howell Mountain Cabernet. He went to the bar, opened the bottle, and poured some wine into a large Riedel wineglass. No better glassware to really enjoy a great wine. He was pleased with his choice: a medium to full body, with deep aromas of blackberry, red currant and some chalk. He loved that about big American wine, and the moderate tannins made this one a perfect pick.

He was not very hungry, and decided to wait and have a bite of his leftover Indian food from the night before at home. He slowly got up from the bar and walked toward the young *couple finishing their meal. They looked ecstatic.*

"How was your dinner tonight?" asked Chef Dewey with a smile.

"Absolutely fantastic!" the young man responded. "We are big fans. Could we get a picture with you, please?"

"That would be my pleasure," the chef replied. "Tom, could you take a picture of the three of us please?" he asked his waiter.

"Absolutely, Chef," Tom said.

Chef Bob Dewey put himself between the young couple, offering his photo-op smile. He loved doing that; he loved the fact that many of those pictures were going to be framed and displayed in the homes of his guests.

After the waiter took the picture, Chef Dewey told the newlyweds, "Dessert is on the house. It will be here shortly."

Delighting in their enthusiastic smiles, he decided to leave for home.

He said good night to his crew and left the remaining wine in the bottle, telling his staff that he would be in Miami and New York for the next few weeks. Going back to his office he took off the chef coat, picked up his jacket and left through the back door of the restaurant. As he was walking toward his car, he felt his appetite for the Indian food growing. He decided to take the highway home tonight, a change in his driving habits, which usually consisted of enjoying the 2:00 a.m. traffic jam on the Strip. His stomach started to growl as he entered I-15 and took a right on the Las Vegas Beltway heading north.

His house was located in a new development called Canyon Lake, in the northwest part of town. It was a big house, and he enjoyed the large kitchen and the pool in the backyard. He hosted some amazing parties, which many celebrities were eager to attend because of the superior quality of the catering and wine. He was listening to KJUL 104.5 FM to hear some oldies, and he suddenly felt tired. Granted, it was 2:15 a.m., but he started to realize that he was not a young man anymore. Maybe he should slow down a little bit. The thought of not cooking, not working the line, came out as fast as it came in.

"No way! Life is too short!" he said, his loud voice filling the car.

And then he started to sing along with Dean Martin to "Just in Time," entering his neighborhood as the end of the song faded out.

****

The Handler was waiting for the chef in his kitchen, having no problem getting into a house protected by a security alarm that he knew how to disengage. A big park was right behind the huge house, but he was not worried about people seeing him, as it was so dark at this late hour. He had only to jump the fence, making sure not to leave any trace behind him.

The house was sumptuous, a prime example of the best of Mediterranean architecture. The horseshoe driveway brought you to a front door of iron and glass. Strategically posted lights gave a classy look to the big empty house. The landscape was without a doubt done by professionals, offering a beautiful Spanish fountain in the front yard and a majestic one in the back that fed into what seemed like an Olympic-size pool. Italian stone paths meandered from an immense terrace equipped with a wood pizza oven, a dream barbecue, a full bar and all the gadgets a chef could desire. Custom French furniture and lounge chairs completed the decoration of the patio, and the gorgeous view of the blue pool was phenomenal in the moonlight.

But the most impressive room in the house was the kitchen. The owner, a world-class chef, had opted for a professional look, with stainless steel everywhere. In the middle of the room was a medium-size cooking island, with ten burners, two convection gas units, a twenty-four-inch grill and a thirty-six inch flat top. An immense hood hung over the island, filled with hooks bearing well-polished copper pots and pans. On the right were a huge walk-in fridge and a separate walk-in freezer that had enough room to hold food for a dinner at the White House. A long, thick butcher table was on the left side of the room, with incredible space for food prep. Big mobile cabinets came down from the ceiling, holding all the pantry items. There was also a deep sink with three compartments next to a commercial dishwasher that finished your dishes in three minutes, not forty-five. Overall, it was very impressive. The Handler made a note to himself to get one of those dishwashers for his wife. He would have plenty of cash to spend after this job.

The Handler had come to this same house a few months before, when his so-called duck was in Florida working in the restaurant he owned there. After studying the surroundings for hours at that time, the Handler had designed a floor plan of the house, just in case he had to make a quick escape. He didn't think that would be necessary. After a few minutes of appreciating the kitchen, he took some tools from his briefcase and positioned them on the wood table. He placed a large white plastic tarp by the sink, brought in a chair from the luxurious living room, installed it in the center of the kitchen and sat down. He looked at his watch: 2:10 a.m.

Ten minutes passed, and silence was welcome in this immense kitchen. It was the calm before the storm. The fridge and freezer humming in the background were the only sounds in the room. Suddenly, the Handler saw the lights of a car as it drove past the front of the house. A few seconds later he heard the garage door opening. He slowly closed his eyes. His hands were sweating inside his latex gloves, but his concentration was maximal. He knew exactly how things were going to happen.

He heard the chef drop his car keys in a glass bowl in the main entrance, and then his shoes on the marble floor as he walked toward the kitchen. The steps were getting closer and closer. The Handler rose from his chair, picked up his PPK .22, put on the silencer and pointed the gun toward what was now a dark shadow at the entrance of the room.

As Bob Dewey entered the kitchen and turned on the lights he startled, jumping back more in surprise than fear. Obviously, he was not expecting anybody; his wife was in New York. In the next instant his hands went to his heart. He started to show fear as soon as he saw the gun with the silencer in front of his eyes.

"Who the hell are you?" the chef demanded. "What are you doing in my house? Get out before I call the cops!" The chef was trying to gain control but still wore a terrified expression.

"Sit down, Chef Dewey," said the Handler. "I have a message for you. Keep quiet. Don't do anything stupid, or I will shoot you in the leg right now." He kept his piece aimed higher up though.

"What do you want?" asked the chef, his voice lower. "Money? I have money. I can give you anything you want."

"Sit on this chair and put your hands behind your back."

There was no way for the chef to escape, as the Handler was pointing the gun right at his heart. Looking around, the chef started to slowly walk toward the chair in the center of the kitchen, as ordered. The Handler had anticipated the man would try to defend himself, of course. He watched as the chef caught sight of the beautiful block of Messermeister knives, imagining the man must have used them countless times in that glorious kitchen. Now, in what was doubtless a split second of despair, the chef threw himself in the direction of the knives, grabbing the first one he could reach and turning to throw it at the Handler. But the Handler was too fast and too skilled for a mere amateur. Before the chef could launch the knife a shot released, the sound muffled by the silencer, and the Handler watched the chef crumple in pain, grabbing his right knee. He dropped the knife on the floor, and before he could move again, the Handler *was at his side leaning over him, pulling him to his feet, shoving him into the chair and handcuffing him. All of this took place in a matter of less than ten seconds.*

"That was really stupid of you, Chef," the Handler hissed. "It seems to me you want to do it the hard way."

As he sealed the chef's mouth with duct tape, he could hear the man moaning in pain and see the terrified look in his eyes. The Handler didn't care.

Blood from the chef's knee started to pool on the plastic tarp covering the Italian white marble. The Handler stepped back to the table, grabbed his PPK .22 with the silencer still on it and put it back in his vest.

"Now, Chef, you must be wondering who I am and what I want," the Handler said.

Chef Dewey's eyes bulged in terror, his breathing a panicked pant.

"I have been hired by a party who has had enough of you and your profession," the Handler continued. "I do not know exactly what their grievances are, and to be honest, I really don't care. You are going to die tonight. I'm sorry."

He paused for a moment, adding, "I want you to know that I enjoy all your business ventures, your cooking and your personality on TV. This is nothing personal. It is a shame, yes, but perhaps it's also time to pass the torch to the younger generation."

The Handler went to the table and picked up a small, sharp knife. He brought it to the mouth of the chef and carved a small hole in the duct tape, just between his lips. Some sounds came out of the chef's mouth.

"No, no! Please, I did not do anything wrong! Please let me live!" the chef begged.

The Handler ignored the pleas, went back to the table and put the knife on it.

"I have money! Take whatever you want, but please

don't kill me!" the chef continued to beg through the little hole in the tape. The panic in his voice was full blown. The Handler moved around the table, surveying his tools for the night: a funnel, a plastic container, the knife, a piece of metal and a three-foot-long tube.

"Now, we are going to have some fun, Chef!"

Chapter 3

As the night started to slow down, I decided to hand the responsibilities to our sous-chef, Kamondo Baka. I knew he loved the task. There were still quite a few tickets on the rail, but he could handle it without any problems. A native of Kenya, Kamondo had studied in England and worked in a British pub. He was really good, and all the other cooks respected him. Moose and I agreed that Kamondo could easily take the spot of executive chef whenever I was too busy solving crimes and Moose had to step down from the line work.

"Take over, Kamondo," I said.

"Yes, Chef," he said, stepping in like the pro sous-chef that he was.

I adjusted my coat and apron, washed my hands and entered the dining room. It was still packed, filled with a vibrant crowd. The liquor, wine and beer were starting to have their effect on our guests, and a fantastic atmosphere reigned at the restaurant. Patrons were smiling, joking with servers and having a great time. I went to the bar, got a glass of cranberry juice and started to walk around the tables, talking to people.

Many regulars were there, and it was always a great pleasure to see them. As I was not in all the time, I took the opportunity to catch up with them, listening to their stories and sharing mine.

"Good evening, Dr. Clark, Mrs. Clark. Good to see you tonight," I said.

"Sebastien, put down your juice and go get a wineglass," said Dr. Clark. "I have a bottle from Peter Michael, a 2010 Chardonnay Point Rouge. Come and try it ... you'll love it!"

"Be right back," I said, returning to the bar for a Riedel Chardonnay glass.

I couldn't miss tasting that wine. Dr. Clark was a fan of this winery located in Sonoma County, just a few miles from the northern part of Napa Valley, north of Calistoga, California. I had discovered some amazing wines from that winery, thanks to him.

"This wine has the typical rich honeysuckle Chardonnay flavors that will coat your mouth," Dr. Clark said when I sat down at their table. "You will get aromas of ripe apple, dried apricot and candied pineapple, along with notes of coconut, vanilla and crème brûlée." He poured the wine in my glass.

I swirled the wine around the glass a few times, looking at the "legs of the wine," as we called it. The legs, also known as "tears of wine," was a good indicator of the alcohol content. This Peter Michael was at 15.3 percent, which was pretty high, but, man, was it full of amazing flavors. I sniffed with my right nostril, swirled the wine again, sniffed with my left nostril and then took a sip.

"Wow, this is intense!" I said. "I can even get a hint of white truffle." I took another sip. "Thank you for sharing your prize with me. I am a big fan of Mr. Michael, thanks to you," I said with a smile.

We chit-chatted a little bit more and then I stood up, thanked them again for the wine, and moved on to other tables.

All the customers seemed to be very pleased with the quality of food we'd put out tonight.

"Your Lucky Bucket Certified Evil beer braised veal cheeks were amazing!" one man told me as I looked at the empty plate he had clearly scraped clean. "Your pork liver pâté with pickles was the perfect appetizer with a nice beer. I also had a bite of my wife's scallops with the quinoa cake. Soft as butter, no need for a knife. Thank you for a great experience!"

"No, thank you for coming and supporting us," I said.

"Have a great night."

I looked in the direction of the table where my boss sat with Mayor Daniel Costa, City Councilman Rob Dewars, and a lady I did not recognize.

"Good evening, lady and gentlemen. How was your dinner tonight?" I said as I approached their table.

"Great," said the mayor as he rose from his chair to shake my hand. "You remember Councilman Rod Dewars. You know your boss, and this young lady is Ms. Christine Jones. Christine is from Chicago. She's in charge of organizing the next Omaha Marathon in September," he said, adding, "I know you are a runner, so I thought it would be neat to bring her here."

"Good evening, Ms. Jones," I said, extending my hand to shake hers. She was a very good-looking woman, probably in her late thirties, and she appeared to be in great shape. I figured she must work out in addition to running.

She smiled at me. "I hear you are a busy man," she said. "How can you manage a full-time police job, own a restaurant and be a marathoner?"

"Easy," I replied, "Detective work for the paycheck, restaurant for the good wine and great food and running to forget and lose all of the above!" I laughed.

They all smiled.

It was true that I had started to run because I was getting a little heavy. I wasn't vain; I just didn't feel as good with the extra weight. I felt good about my looks otherwise, though: my hair was still dark and thick and curly, I had strong features, olive skin that tanned easily and dark eyes that had melted more than one lady's heart. For that I thanked my maternal grandfather, who emigrated from Northern Italy to France, bringing his charm as well as his good looks. I liked having two different countries' blood flowing through my veins; it made me feel like I had superpowers. After all, how else could I be a full-time detective and an executive chef! I chuckled to myself at the last thought. Another thing I enjoyed about running was the way it encouraged my mind to meander. For the most part, though, as I'd just told my guests, I ran because it gave me a good excuse to continue having amazing meals with friends and family, without feeling bad about having an extra glass or an extra bite. Plus, once you've run your first marathon, you never want to stop. It's as addictive as good food, good wine and good … anything.

My boss and his tablemates were done with their third bottle of wine, getting ready for dessert. I offered them a round of after-dinner drinks, said my good-byes and left them to plan the race.

The Omaha Marathon had become a huge success for the city and I was eager to run it again. It was great to run in my own town. The organization of the event was intense, as the police had to block numerous streets downtown and there were water stations every few miles. Volunteers and supporters were everywhere, cheering the runners on. There were even bands playing music in the streets at eight o'clock on Sunday morning. The marathon went on for many miles, but it was definitely a lot of fun too. My last marathon was 26.2 miles, in Paris, just a few months ago. Paris was my original hometown and I still had family there.

So, how did a Frenchman end up in Omaha, Nebraska? I moved from France to the United States when I was fifteen years old. My dad, a French Air Force colonel, had been posted at the OFFUTT in Bellevue, Nebraska. The family lived in West Omaha, not on base. My dad drove to the base every day when he was in town. But often he was away, traveling to the various air force bases scattered across the country. There was a Franco-American partnership taking place at the time: the development of the concept of drones.

My sister and I soon became the "gamins américains" to all our family in France. Since then, Omaha has become my hometown. I graduated from Millard Dodgers High School and then went on to college, earning a bachelor's degree in criminology at the University of Nebraska–Omaha. I always knew I wanted to work in law enforcement. After graduating, I decided to get a master's in criminology and criminal justice from the University of Maryland. My years on the East Coast were a lot of fun, and the university had one of the best programs in the country. At the end of my two years, I was offered an FBI position as translator in Quantico, Virginia, but I decided to come back to Omaha and work for the OPD. I still loved my town, which was constantly changing and getting bigger and better, but I also was in love with Marie, now my ex-wife.

I headed back to the kitchen, planning to wrap up for the night and then go home. It was a typical Saturday night, and I was grateful for how busy we'd been and how happy all our customers were.

Unbeknownst to me, the night was anything but typical—I was about to be thrown into one of the most convoluted cases of my career as a detective.

Chapter 4

As I walked back to the kitchen, my phone started to vibrate. I stopped, took it out of my pocket, and saw Marie's number. What now? Was Tom in trouble?

"Hi, Marie," I said into the phone. "What's going on? Is Tom okay?" I asked, wondering why she was calling me on a Saturday night when she knew I was working at the restaurant.

"No, Seb, it's not Tom. It's something else. Hold on … I'll be right back."

While I waited for Marie to get back on the line, I started thinking about her. About us. That happened whenever she called. I'd always get a mix of memories. Happy times. Regretted failures.

Marie and I had been married for ten years when she got fed up with my busy 24/7 professional life as a police detective and an executive chef. After many hours of marriage counseling, she decided to divorce me. I knew I was not the best husband, as I was working all the time. She was afraid I would get shot on the job, sever my hand in the kitchen, or have a heart attack from the stress of trying to do both. She could not take it anymore. We decided to part, but we remained friends. In the course of our tumultuous relationship we had a son, Thomas Daniel Saint-Gemmes, now sixteen and a sophomore in high school.

Marie was a business lawyer at a local firm that specialized in licensing. She was very successful in everything she did. Our divorce was pretty much the only failure she'd had in her life. Everything she touched or did turned out to be an achievement. She was a Nebraska native, born and bred in

Lincoln, and we met while attending the University of Nebraska–Omaha. She was majoring in international law, and we fell for each other. She later told me it was my accent that caught her attention in class. We dated for a few years, long distance while I was in Maryland, and got married in Omaha. She was the one who pushed me to get a diploma in culinary arts, as she loved what I was cooking at home.

I became an American citizen, and she became a French citizen later on. She, Tom and I all now have dual citizenship. I often told Marie that I wished there were a country where the best of both our countries could merge: the American work ethic and the French joie de vivre. Can you imagine that? Perfection…

The French good life definitely included food. It had always been important in my life, as my mother and grandmothers were stellar cooks. They transformed any type of fare into a delicious meal. My mom would open the fridge at home, take out all the leftovers and create a three-star meal out of it. She had some great teachers: her paternal grandmother owned a little bistro in Châteauroux, in the center of France, and her own mother had to prepare food for six children while the family lived in a tiny apartment in the suburbs of Paris. This virus was passed on to me. I always enjoyed the smell of garlic, toasted bread, roasted leg of lamb—all of it. … That was why, after being on the force for four years, I decided to take Marie's advice and go back to school part-time at the CIO. I already had most of the core courses so all I had to do were the actual cooking courses and restaurant management classes. I tried to squeeze the classes into my hectic daily work schedule; and, after four years, I finally graduated. This was thanks to the faculty's letting me off the hook many times when I was called to the scene of a homicide or some other crime. My instructors would always let me make up classes; and, even today, I still feel grateful for that.

As I said, Moose and I met at the CIO, and we hit it off right away. He graduated the year before I did, and he started to work in a restaurant to get his feet wet. We knew we wanted to open a restaurant together, but I had to finish the program first. During that year we worked on Sundays, creating a business plan and doing all that it takes to start a company. My dream of opening a restaurant was passed on to me by my family; but, unfortunately, despite her initial encouragement, Marie did not remain patient with me and my goals. To be honest with you, she was right; she pretty much raised Tom on her own, and I have always given her credit for that.

The memories kept flooding my mind while I waited for Marie to get back on the phone. More happy times. More regretted failures. After a busy night in the restaurant, I was not in the mood for all this reverie.

Marie! Why are you calling if it's not about Tom? I didn't say that aloud of course. What I did say was "Marie, are you there? What's going on?" I didn't attempt to mask my irritation.

"Sorry, Seb … I didn't mean to keep you holding that long." Her voice on the other end of the line sounded fragile.

"What's wrong?" I asked, my tone filling with concern as I heard her start to cry.

"I just got a call from Elizabeth Dewey in New York," Marie said, sniffling. "She needs to talk to you, Seb. Bob is dead."

"What did you say?" I sputtered, starting to shake.

Marie was sobbing on the other end.

"Tell me what happened," I told her, forcing myself to stay focused so that I could calm her down.

I heard Marie take a few deep breaths, and then she said, "Bob was murdered in some horrible way."

"Where did it happen?" I asked, my initial shock ebbing as my detective's instincts kicked in.

"In their house in Las Vegas," Marie replied.

We talked for a few more minutes, until I was sure that Marie was calmer and would be okay, and then we said good night.

That was the end of my supposed typical Saturday night.

Chapter 5

After only a few hours of sleep I woke up, took a quick shower, made coffee, threw on some clothes and jumped into my car, headed for the station.

The OPD building was located downtown, only a few blocks from the restaurant. Traffic was very easy on I-80, and I arrived in ten minutes. It usually took twenty-five to forty-five minutes to get from my house in the Westside suburb to downtown Omaha, but that was during typical rush-hour traffic.

I was still processing the small amount of information that Marie had given me about Bob's murder the night before. I'd tried to call Elizabeth right after I got off the phone with Marie, but there was no answer at any of the Dewey's numbers in New York. I left Elizabeth a voice-mail message, telling her I would call back in the morning. I figured I might as well wait to do that from the police station, so I could immediately start looking into whatever she told me over the phone.

I pulled into the parking lot, got out of the car and headed toward the five-story OPD building. The homicide department was located on the third floor, and I always made sure to walk up and down the stairs instead of taking the elevator. The OPD was close to the courthouse, right on Dodge Street, the key artery of the city. The construction dated from the post-war era. It had a very nice façade, with a lot of interesting architectural characteristics. The inside of the building was the complete opposite though. As soon as you entered, you saw nothing but state-of-the-art security equipment everywhere. Officers were always on duty in the main entryway, ready to scan people coming in and out of the building. The booking department was located directly to the left of the entrance.

As I entered the building, I took in all the familiar surroundings. A few tired-looking hookers were sitting on the bench, in the company of some drunks. The latter were fast asleep, heads down. Together, they represented the leftovers of downtown Saturday-night partying. This *was* a typical Sunday morning at OPD.

I showed my badge to the officer on duty, Robert Bista, and climbed the stairs, two at a time, to the third floor. Only a few people were in the room, so it looked like it was a pretty calm Saturday night, at least as far as homicides were concerned.

I nodded to my fellow detectives. "Good morning, gentlemen," I said. "How are we doing? Anything exciting during the shift?"

"Not really," Detective Burton answered. "Just a shooting in North O. A drive-by. Nobody hurt, but a lot of damage to houses and cars. They used an automatic weapon; we believe it's gang related."

I shrugged as I sat down at my desk.

Burton looked at me. "What are you doing here, anyway?" he asked. "I thought this was your day off. Can't get enough of us, it looks like," he finished with a grin.

"I wish that were the case," I said, turning on my computer. "A friend of mine was killed in Las Vegas on Friday night and I need to get more info."

"That's rough. Let us know if we can help."

"Thanks."

"Busy night at the restaurant last night?"

"Packed. The chief was there with the mayor."

"Nice! I smell a promotion."

"Not interested right now, way too busy. Sorry guys, let's talk later. I need to call New York."

As the guys all turned back toward their respective computers, I picked up the receiver of the phone on my desk and dialed the Dewey's home number in New York.

Elizabeth picked up after the third ring. "Hello?" She sounded exhausted.

"Good morning, Elizabeth," I said. "It's Sebastien Saint-Gemmes. How are you feeling this morning?" I kept my voice soft and reassuring.

"Good morning, Sebastien. I got your voice mail. Thank you. I could not reach you last night, so I called Marie. I don't know what to say at this point. I-I-I'm devastated. ... I don't know what to do or what to even think. I booked a flight to Vegas, so I'm leaving in two hours. I was hoping you could meet me out there. Maybe you'll be able to help me understand the situation and figure out why Bob was killed."

"Yes, of course, Elizabeth. Bob was not just a good friend to me; he was also a mentor. I will get on a flight today and meet you in Vegas tonight." I was sure Southwest would have a non-stop flight from Omaha to Las Vegas. I just needed to get things squared away with my current case, clear it with my bosses at OPD and then let Moose know. "I will call you as soon as I land in Vegas, Elizabeth," I said. "Please keep your cell on."

"All right. Thank you again," she said. "If you don't mind, I'd prefer to meet you at the morgue. I need some time alone with Bob."

"Of course," I said.

She said good-bye, crying as she hung up the phone.

I hung up too, leaning back in my chair, trying to understand who would want to kill my old friend. Bob and I first met here in Omaha ten years ago, when Moose and I opened our restaurant. Bob Dewey was a good friend of Patsy Williams, who won the James Beard Foundation Award for Outstanding Restaurant two years in a row. Patsy owned La Cigale, a South of France eatery rated two stars in the Michelin Guide. La Cigale was just down the street from the Drunken Frog. Patsy was a local, and Omaha was thrilled to have one of its own as a star in the global food industry. She was also the author of some best-selling cookbooks. For two seasons she had been in a series on the Food Network, *True Food Origin*. Chef Bob Dewey and Master Chef Pierre LeJeune from Chicago had been her co-stars. Moose, Patsy and I had become good friends, as we all were in the industry and our restaurants were so close to each other. We would go to her place after the dinner service, or she would bring her crew to our place. We'd have a few glasses of wine together and laugh and talk about our respective nights. We also often hung out at local fund-raising events, where good food was a popular draw. I needed to call Patsy and Chef LeJeune to let them know the situation.

Above all, I had to call the Las Vegas Metropolitan Police Department to get some information about the crime scene. I was lucky enough to have met a detective from Sin City while attending an important law enforcement convention a year or so ago. My partner during my class sessions during that week was Detective Erica Hunter. She was a rising star in the LVMPD, and we hit it off right away, becoming fast friends. We remained in contact after the conference, and even now, a year later, we were still in touch.

I dialed the main number for the LVMPD.

When the switchboard picked up, I said, "Good morning. Detective Erica Hunter, please. This is Detective Sebastien Saint-Gemmes from the Omaha PD."

I knew that Erica would be at work today. She was a workaholic. When she wasn't working, she preferred to spend her time in a good restaurant, not a bar. We were a lot alike: both loved our work, our food and our runs. I had dialed the switchboard as opposed to her direct line, just in case she was out in the field.

The line crackled and then I heard Erica's voice.

"Detective Hunter speaking. What can I do for you?"

"Erica, hello. This is Sebastien Saint-Gemmes, 'your only French friend,' as you like to say. How are you?"

"Sebbi, my dear! The desk butchered your name." She laughed. "How are you? I'm so happy to hear from you. What brings you to me? You're working on a Sunday morning … no cooking last night?"

"Very long night; but, yes, I am at the station right now. Erica, I am calling you about the murder of Chef Bob Dewey from Tartufo at the Callegio."

"Right here on my desk. I am the detective in charge," she said. "The case is already steaming here in Vegas, so it will be national news by noon central time, for sure."

"Erica, I need a favor," I said. "Chef Bob Dewey was a dear friend of mine, and his widow has asked me to be involved in solving the murder. I could really help you with this case. I know how to talk to crews in restaurants and hotels. I will just be an observer; I understand I have no jurisdiction in Vegas. What do you say?"

I had told Erica all about my restaurant and passion for cooking; she knew I was a certified executive chef.

Erica was quiet on the other end of the line. After a moment or two, she said, "All right, Seb. It might not be a bad idea to have someone from the industry on this one. You can help translate the hospitality jargon."

"Thank you, Erica. I'll get my boss to okay things on this end."

"Sounds good," she said. "By the way, did you know that Chef Dewey died as a result of suffocation?"

"How?" I asked, surprised. "The coroner was able to tell you that already?"

"The body is with a medical examiner at the coroner's office. The ME hasn't completed the autopsy yet, but I could tell right away the man was suffocated. I saw it with my own eyes yesterday when we got to the crime scene," she said.

"How?" I asked again.

"Someone shoved mashed grain down his throat. He suffocated on a mixture of corn and water."

"That's sickening," I said.

"Weird too," she said. "Any ideas who would do something like that?"

I did have some ideas, but I kept them to myself. I wasn't going to share until I was sure.

Chapter 6

After hanging up the phone I called my boss, who approved my taking a few days off to go to Vegas to work with the LVMPD. I booked a non-stop flight to Las Vegas, leaving from Omaha at 4:20 p.m. It was a three-hour flight, so I calculated that I should arrive in Sin City by 5:20 p.m. Pacific Time. I arranged for a rental car and then made a reservation at a hotel on West Charleston Boulevard in Vegas, just a few miles from the crime scene. I did not know exactly how long I would be in Vegas, but I planned to be back in Omaha by Tuesday night, arranging my schedule at the OPD and the restaurant accordingly. Another detective would cover for me, and we had no parties planned at the restaurant, so when I called to tell Moose I was going to Vegas, he assured me it would be fine.

That left me with two more calls to make. I shifted to my cell phone, opened Contacts, scrolled to a Chicago number and called it.

After a few rings it went to voice mail: "Hello, you have reached Pierre LeJeune. Please leave a message; I will get back to you as soon as possible."

I waited to hear the customary beep, and then I spoke into the phone. "Hello, Chef. This is Chef Sebastien Saint-Gemmes from the Drunken Frog in Omaha. I'm a friend of Patsy Williams and Bob Dewey. Please give me a call when you have a second. There's been an accident and I need to talk to you as soon as possible. Thank you, and have a good day."

I ended the call, and my thoughts centered on this amazing master chef I'd had the pleasure of meeting a few times at some fund-raising events in Omaha. Pierre LeJeune was an older gentleman, but he was at the top of his game, one of the few certified master chefs in the country. He owned Celadon, a beautiful high-end restaurant in downtown Chicago where he offered a full menu based on molecular gastronomy, the food science that studies the physical and chemical transformations of ingredients that occur during the cooking process. Fascinating stuff. I had visited his place a few times, and each time I was amazed. His level of creativity was astounding. He offered fourteen courses and not a simple item among them. Everything I tasted was simply exquisite. Not a cheap place to eat, but the restaurant was booked with reservations six months in advance. I hoped Chef LeJeune would call me back soon.

Scrolling through Contacts again, I opened Patsy Williams's entry. I did not want to tell her that her friend, Bob Dewey, had been murdered, but I had to do it. I called the number for La Cigale. I knew full well they were closed on Sunday, but I also knew Patsy liked to be on her own in the kitchen on her day off, practicing some specials for the weeks ahead.

Patsy was the Nebraska equivalent of Alice Cooper from Chez Panisse in California. She had a charisma that made all the cooks and chefs in town display immense respect for her. At five foot two she was tiny, but she was also formidable, and most people treated her as they would a beloved aunt. In addition to our socializing, Patsy had invited me to help her create some dishes a few times. We prepared roasted lamb tenderloin stuffed with fresh goat cheese, sun-dried tomatoes and a julienne of blanched spinach and carrots. It was amazing! So was the wine we drank in the kitchen while making it. We served the lamb on an Israeli couscous croquette, and made a simple fresh blueberry gastrique, too. We seared the meat on all sides and finished it in the oven. It was medium rare, and we let it rest a good five minutes before slicing it. I had brought a bottle of Côte-Rôtie from the Rhône wine region of France to pair with the meal; the same bottle we opened as we were cooking. The wine was a 2001 Guigal Château d'Ampuis, rated 95 points by Robert Parker. It was a 100 percent Syrah (also known as Shiraz), with flavors of black currant, blackberry, coffee and bacon fat. The tannins had softened with time, and it paired so well with the lamb. Those memories and exchanges with Chef Patsy Williams will stay with me as one of my best meals.

The answering machine at the restaurant picked up, so I knew Patsy was screening calls.

"Hi, Chef. This is Sebastien from the Drunken Frog. Please pick up ... I need to talk to you—it is important."

"Hi, Sebastien!" Patsy said in a pleasant voice. "What's up?"

"Patsy, I have some bad news. I'm on my way to Las Vegas. Chef Bob Dewey is dead. Someone murdered him. His wife, Elizabeth, has asked me to help her find out what's going on."

"Oh no-o-o-o!" Patsy said, starting to cry. "Not Bob! Why? Do they know who did it? How did he die? Tell me, Sebastien. I want to know. ..."

"I know you have plenty of questions Patsy, but I don't have the answers now," I said. "I will call you in the morning when I know more. I just wanted to inform you."

"Okay, call me in the morning. ASAP, please," she said.

"I will. I promise to keep in touch. Talk to you later," I said, ending the call.

I had a few answers already, but I did not have the courage to share them with Patsy yet.

As I was driving to the airport, my mind could not stop racing. This murder was beyond bizarre. It was twisted, sick. Someone had stuffed mashed corn and water down the throat of the victim; enough to suffocate the man to death. The killer was communicating a vicious message, one that he or she took seriously enough to make Chef Bob Dewey suffer, and then display that suffering to the world.

After half an hour of preliminary TSA inspections, I boarded the plane on time. We were in the air just a few minutes after taking our seats. I had three hours to rest on the plane before beginning what I knew would be an intense night in Las Vegas. My sleep the previous night had been short, and I felt exhaustion kick in as soon as I heard the flight attendant announce that beverages were going to be served in a few moments. I closed my eyes and tried to avoid thinking too much about what was waiting for me.

Chapter 7

The Handler luxuriated in his newly rented Mercedes S Class Coupe, enjoying his drive east. He had just crossed the Colorado border, having left Las Vegas on Sunday morning after a great evening. He planned to be in Denver on Monday, for what he thought of as "the meeting." Driving along I-70, he began reflecting on the past twenty-four hours.

After finishing his job at around four in the morning, he decided to take a long nap and then enjoy the Strip. He did a little more gambling, and then went to the seven o'clock show of KÀ Cirque du Soleil. He enjoyed the acrobatics, and respected those performers for hanging on a rope ten feet in the air, with no protection. They were so good at entertaining crowds of people looking for the ultimate thrill—vicariously, of course. These performers had to train for hours and hours just to execute the perfect move that one time; if that move had a single tiny flaw, death would follow.

The Handler began to compare himself to the acrobats. His need to move with perfection was different, but he enjoyed the extreme training and preparation necessary for his own work, and that enjoyment—that respect for the rigorous training—added to his enjoyment of the show.

He had planned for his own show for well over a year, in fact, complete with many rehearsals. His employer was paying a lot of money to achieve whatever the end goal was, which the Handler didn't know ... and didn't care to know. In the meantime, he decided to enjoy Vegas "to the max," as it were, by indulging himself with good wines, good food, nice cars, great hotels and, occasionally, women.

After the show he had a reservation for dinner at Le Comptoir, a restaurant owned by a world-famous French chef, Jacques de Montaigne, who never actually worked in the kitchen anymore. The Handler decided to try the chef's franchise at the MCM. He'd been to the one in Paris the year before, and he'd had a great time and great food. That was in Rue de Roche, in the seventeenth district of the French capital. The restaurant concept was based on the open kitchen, where patrons could see what the chefs were preparing for the evening. It was not a new concept anymore, but Le Comptoir had been the pioneer of it twenty-odd years ago.

The Handler still thought of it fondly. He remembered the full experience: appetizer, main entrée and dessert, all paired with wine, all of it vegetarian. The appetizer was a beautiful in-house Norwegian smoked tofu. It was served with some fresh fried potato-dill gaufrettes, a drizzle of extra-virgin olive oil called Elixir de Nicolas from a local producer in the South of France, organic lemon from the town of Menton on the Italian border near Ventimiglia, and freshly made crème fraîche. The tofu had been cured like a gravlax with a mixture of salt, pepper, sugar and dill for four days, and then was rinsed of its coating. It was sliced to perfection and surprisingly had a great similarity to the smoked salmon. The main entrée consisted of braised seaweeds, served with a delicate morel truffle oil cream sauce. The taste of the mushrooms and the iodine flavor of the seaweed created an amazing burst of flavors in his mouth. He drank a wonderful white Sancerre with dinner. The Sauvignon Blanc was crisp, with a hint of green apple and even some melon, a perfect fit for the experience. To finish, the Handler had a café gourmand, which was an espresso served alongside three miniature desserts, or "bites." There was a chocolate truffle, an orange biscotti and an almond shortbread. It was a perfect evening, right there in front of the kitchen crew. After dinner he had a very nice walk in the Parc Monceau.

As he entered the restaurant in Vegas all he hoped for was to not be disappointed with the American version. He heard the chef in Vegas had been trained in France and previously worked at Le Comptoir in Tokyo. The Handler was seated, and he opened the menu. After reading for a few minutes he put it down in disgust. Now he was upset: the Las Vegas menu was almost identical to the one in Paris. He dropped his napkin on the table just as the waiter was coming back to take his order.

"Everything all right, sir?"

"No. I am very disappointed with your selections. I dined at your Parisian sister eatery and it was almost the same menu. It is inexcusable for an establishment like yours. Sorry, but I am leaving."

The Handler could not understand why a world-famous chef would do the same menu in each of his restaurants around the world. The concept was very good, but he had hoped for a twist, with the specialties of that country in each Le Comptoir, not the same dishes as in Paris. The executive chef in Vegas had amazing talent, as a graduate of the Culinary Institute of America—or perhaps it was Johnson and Wales, he wasn't sure. He should be more than capable of bringing some diversity and specials to the menu, in the Handler's opinion. He knew that hundreds of apprentice cooks would do everything possible to learn the trade of Chef Jacques de Montaigne.

With the server standing at the table, speechless, the Handler walked to the front of the restaurant, asked for his coat from the coat check, and did not even tip the young lady who handed it to him. He walked through the hotel lobby, exited, and hailed a cab.

He already knew where he would have dinner: Tartufo at the Callegio.

He'd heard recently that the foie gras was grade A quality, and he smiled to himself at the thought.

Chapter 8

The plane landed on time at McCarran International, the airport serving Las Vegas and its environs. I had not checked any bags, as I was only planning to stay for two days. I made sure to fit a suit and some nice shirts in my carry-on, so that I could dress appropriately when indulging in some of the best culinary spots of Sin City.

This was not my first visit to Vegas. My family had visited the city on vacation two years before we moved to Omaha. The town was not what it was today. Downtown, with the Howdy, Partner cowboy sign, was still the main emblem of the city at that time; and Fantasy Land was the spot to stay on the Strip. I remember eating with my parents at those crazy buffets where all-you-can-eat lobster cost no more than ten dollars. Things have changed! Today, chefs from all around the world fought to open their latest concepts, and hotels did their best to accommodate them by building more casinos all over town. I had to admit, though, as a twelve-year-old growing up in France and dreaming of the United States, while driving along Fremont Street and seeing the lights of the casinos, or walking on an air-conditioned sidewalk in the middle of summer, I did wonder what would come next.

My second visit to Vegas, many years later, was for the law enforcement convention where I'd met Erica. The Strip looked nothing like I remembered. It was all new, filled with amazing construction.

This trip was completely different from either of the other two. Now I had to find information on, and clues to, the murder of my friend. I shuddered at the thought.

As I walked through the airport, headed toward the rental cars, I took out my phone and called Erica. She didn't answer, so I waited for voice mail.

"Hi, this is Sebastien. I just arrived. I'm going to the coroner's office to meet Elizabeth Dewey. I am hoping you and I can have dinner at Rocco in the Palm Grove Resort and Casino tonight. Please call me when you can, and we can make plans. Thanks."

There was only one person in front of me at the rental place, so I decided to call Elizabeth to let her know that I was on my way.

"Hello," she said softly.

"Elizabeth, this is Sebastien. I just arrived. I wanted to make sure you were still at the coroner's office."

"Yes, I'm here."

"All right. I will be there in a few minutes. I have the address."

"I'll wait for you, Sebastien," she said, clearly holding back a sob.

I ended the call and put my phone in my pocket just as the lady in front of me was done taking possession of her keys. I had rented a basic sedan, as I was travelling on my own budget. I wanted to be independent of Erica in case I decided to investigate on my own. The clerk showed me where to get the car, and after taking the keys I crossed the main road to the parking lot. I was amazed by the number of limos passing in front of me. Perhaps I would get one the next time. Las Vegas did that to you: no matter the circumstances of your trip, as soon you arrived you felt like a millionaire!

GPS took me to Pinto Lane via the Las Vegas Beltway, not far from downtown. The trip was going to take only twenty minutes. While driving, I decided to call Tom to wish him good luck on his exam the following morning. It was his first exam of the new school year, and he was nervous about it. Marie had mentioned this to me at the end of our call the night before, when I'd engaged her in small talk to try to calm her down.

My son was happy to hear from me.

"When will you take me to Vegas, Dad?" he wanted to know.

"When you turn twenty-one we'll go to Vegas for the weekend, hit some strip clubs. Okay?"

With a laugh, he said, "I'm not waiting till I'm twenty-one, Dad!"

"Okay. Put your mother on the phone."

After talking to Marie, I tried to call Erica again. To my surprise, she answered right away.

"Hi, Sebastien. I got your message a few minutes ago. I called and made a reservation at Rocco for 8:00 p.m."

"Great! I've heard good things about this restaurant. I'm hungry for meat and red wine. I'll see you there. Please bring all the info you have on the case. I need to be brought up to speed. See you tonight, Erica."

She said good-bye, and I put my phone away.

As I was parking my car in front of the coroner's office, I saw Elizabeth waving to me from the entrance of the office. Many people were walking in and out; the place seemed very busy, especially for a Sunday night.

"Good evening, Elizabeth," I said, hugging her.

"Oh, Sebastien, thank you so much for coming. It means a lot to me. Bob really liked you. He had great respect for you as a person and in both of your careers. He always enjoyed a good Bordeaux with you."

I kissed her on the cheek and hugged her again. She started to cry.

As we walked inside the building a man came toward us.

"I am Dr. Saravoh," he said. "I performed the autopsy. Detective Hunter told me you were coming and that I should give you all the information you need."

"Hello, Doctor. I am Detective Sebastien Saint-Gemmes from the Omaha Police Department."

"Please follow me," he said as he turned down the hall.

"I am going to stay here, Sebastien," Elizabeth said. "You need to have a conversation with the doctor, and I do not want to hear it. I will wait for you right here."

"I will be back soon," I said as I followed the doctor through the large metal doors labeled Morgue.

Closing the doors behind us so that Elizabeth could not hear, he said, "I've had some screwed-up cases in my life, but never anything like this one."

"I know," I said. "The message from the killer is pretty clear. We are exploring the possibility of an animal-rights activist act. Those groups are becoming more and more violent, trying to showcase their cause. Chef Bob Dewey very much enjoyed his meats."

The cold in the room was such a change from the outside temperature that I shivered.

The doctor went to a cabinet, opened it, and pulled out a drawer. A white sheet covered the corpse.

"Are you ready, Detective?"

"As much as I can be," I replied, swallowing hard.

I had seen many corpses in my years as a homicide detective, but it was different to look at the body of a murder victim who was also a friend.

Chef Bob Dewey's eyes were closed, and I could see that his body was already stiff from rigor mortis. But what caught my attention right away were the bruises on his throat.

"Mr. Dewey certainly suffered a great deal. I don't know what kind of sick animal would torture a man like this. When I opened his body, I found more than four pounds of corn in his stomach. The murderer used a three-foot tube and a funnel to pour the mixture into the poor man. His esophagus was completely bruised and scratched. I found some corn in his lungs too. That's what suffocated him. The murderer knew what he was doing. The stomach was full before the lungs were. Sickening. ..."

I tried very hard not to imagine the pain and suffering my friend had gone through.

"There's something else, Detective," said the doctor.

He pulled out the whole drawer and then lifted the sheet from the feet of the dead body. The tag tied around the big toe had Chef Dewey's name on it. I did not notice anything else at first, but then, as the doctor pried apart the toes of the victim, I saw what looked like burned skin.

"What is that, Doc?" I asked.

"Well, at the beginning, I thought it was a scratch. But after examining it with a magnifying glass, here is what I found. Look for yourself."

He handed me the magnifier, and I looked at the mark. After a few seconds I realized there was a letter-shaped form. At first I thought it was a tattoo, but then I realized it *was* a burn mark, just as I had initially thought. Intrigued, I pulled my phone from my vest and took a picture.

"A burn mark? Is that what it is?" I asked, wanting to make sure the doctor and I were on the same page.

"Yes. That's exactly what it is."

"I've never seen a mark like that before," I said.

"I hope you never do again, Detective," said the doctor. "I hope I never do again, either. This man was branded like cattle."

Chapter 9

After talking to Dr. Saravoh I returned to the waiting room, which looked like a hospital cube: all the walls were painted white, with no color except for the seal of the city of Las Vegas. It was a very depressing setting, which did not help the situation in a place where bad news was frequently delivered.

Elizabeth sat in a chair, waiting patiently, just as she'd promised. As I approached her she looked up at me, hungry for information. The problem was that I had more questions in my head than answers. She stood up, so I remained standing.

"Elizabeth, Dr. Saravoh and I talked in detail about what happened to Bob. I need to warn you: it is pretty gruesome."

"Go ahead, Sebastien, tell me; I did not have the nerves or stomach to hear it from Dr. Saravoh before now. He already told me it was disturbing … that's why I wanted you here."

"All right," I said. "Bob died of suffocation as a result of forced ingestion of corn into his lungs. I am so sorry, Elizabeth."

She started sobbing at the news. This was the first she was hearing of the actual cause of death. She had seen Bob's face and the blue marks on his throat, but that was all.

"I saw the blue marks on Bob's throat when I asked to see his face, so I thought he might have been strangled, but suffocation by forced ingestion? I never imagined anything like that, Sebastien. Who could do such a thing? It's so cruel … so vicious. Why would anyone go to such lengths to commit a murder?"

Elizabeth asked the questions rapid-fire, too quickly for me to answer each one. I wasn't sure she expected—or even wanted—the answers in that moment.

"Elizabeth, all I can say at this point is that I do not know—yet. But I do already have some ideas," I said slowly, keeping my voice steady and calm. "Do you feel up to answering some questions?"

"Yes, of course. Anything I can do to help you find whoever did this."

"Good. Did Bob ever receive any threats from some animal-rights activist? Anything that he took seriously, I mean. I know all of us in the food industry have received minor warnings regarding serving certain dishes in our restaurants, but I am talking about something more intense, more violent, in a letter or an e-mail or even a video. Do you recall anything like that?" When she shook her head, I continued. "All right. Do you remember anybody taking pictures of Bob while he was at home or at the restaurant or out shopping for supplies? Any nut case running after him when he was on the Food Network show *True Food Origin,* the one he did with Chef Patsy Williams from Omaha?" When she again shook her head, I pressed her a bit. "Please think hard, Elizabeth. It is very important. Any details you can remember, no matter how insignificant they may seem to you, could help me."

"Nothing really stands out, Sebastien. Bob has been in this business for so long. I remember customers who got mad and complained about the food, like happens in every restaurant. Sometimes meat and fish providers stopped delivering on time, which made it difficult for Bob; but, I don't remember anything violent or crazy or even odd. Certainly he never told me he thought anyone might want to murder him!"

She started to sob again. I had pushed her too hard, too soon.

"Shh," I said softly. "Close your eyes, Elizabeth. Take a few deep breaths. Just relax."

She did what I said, and then after a few moments she froze, as if some memories had just popped into her mind.

Opening her eyes wide, she looked deep into mine. "There actually were two incidents that stood out, Sebastien, but I'd long since forgotten them. Now that we are talking about all this ... I don't know why I forgot. They shocked me at the time."

"It's great you remember, Elizabeth. Take your time. Tell me about the first one."

"Well, the first one was after the lawsuit that Bob faced following a nasty incident at Above the Stars. That was his restaurant at the King Arthur Hotel and Casino here in Vegas. The press was after him for that one. I never did know all the details, but I'm sure you can find information online or in the city archives. Our business attorney, Harold James, whose firm is in Florida, would have the details, too. It was very nasty, the way all lawsuits involving death and money always are." She paused for a few seconds, and I watched her eyes moving as she processed her recollections. "The other incident happened at the Chanterelles restaurant in Miami. This one is more vivid to me, because I was staying in our Florida house when it happened. It was right after the French government refused to send troops to Iraq in 2003 to support the Americans in the quest for Saddam Hussein and his supposed weapons of mass destruction." She paused longer this time, took a deep breath, and looked at me with intense eyes. "We received some pretty threatening letters, phone calls and videos. It was crazy. People were really pumped to hate anything having to do with France. I am sure you remember. Those idiots in Congress were asking to switch the name of French fries to 'freedom fries'—what a bunch of morons." She shook her head sadly. "It was a witch hunt. French wines were poured down the drain, people were throwing rocks at the windows of French restaurants and some suppliers even refused to deliver merchandise to them."

"I remember that time well," I said, interrupting so that she could take a break. "Patsy Williams in Omaha received some weird letters and phones calls at La Cigale. I did not yet have my own restaurant then, but I did some personal investigating to try to help her out. Someone did send her pictures that were taken when she was inside her house. The kind of thing stalkers do to show the victim they are always there, always watching. There were some threatening notes too: 'Go back to France, you coward!'; 'We don't need socialists!'; 'We are watching all you fucking frogs! Beware of where you are going.'" I paused, disgusted by the recollection. After a few seconds I continued. "Even the FBI got involved because of potential terrorism. We eventually found the people responsible for some of the chaos. They were rednecks watching Fox News and getting their heads stuffed with extreme right-wing views. We found out that they had never left the Midwest and had no idea where France was even located!"

"Amazing," Elizabeth said, her voice sad.

"But let's get back to the case now. At that time, with Patsy, a lot of it was just ignorance. What makes you think it was not the same scenario with Bob and Chanterelles?" I asked.

"Well, we got a lot of hate letters, and I agree with you, that could have been more ignorance than anything else. But there was this video that came direct to our home address. It was very disturbing. I'm sure the Miami police department would still have a copy; if not, Harold must have one. Remind me to give you Harold's phone number. I may still even have the number of the detective in charge of the case; his name was José Galantro."

"Yes, I would like to talk to both of them. In the meantime, Elizabeth, can you describe the video to me, please?"

"It was fuzzy at the beginning, but then a clear image appeared, with a flag in the background. And then a man appeared. He wore a black ski mask and some type of camouflage clothing. His voice was altered. It looked like those videos of terrorists with weapons, stating their demands while holding guns. The flag was in the background the entire time. Another guy came on the screen, and they both started to talk about US policies, diminishing the country with their accusations. Then, the man who seemed to be the leader, started to talk about how so-called advanced countries around the world produce their food, how inhumane it is, and so on." Elizabeth slowed down, carefully recalling the details and then relating them to me. "The video shifted to chickens raised by the thousands, so crammed in that they could not walk; poor beaten cows going to slaughterhouses; pigs living in their own filth. There were more disturbing scenes, but the voice was always the same, that altered male voice."

"Elizabeth, you said there was a flag in the background. Do you remember the colors? Or a message, if there was one? Was there any logo or emblem designed on the flag?"

"Give me a second to think," she said as she closed her eyes once again. "Yes, I can see it now. The flag was green and black, and there was something printed in the center of it. I can't remember. ..." She paused, frustrated. "Wait—I can see it now: there was a circle with some lettering inside of it."

"What kind of lettering, Elizabeth?" I asked, probing so she wouldn't lose the mental image.

"It's kind of fuzzy, Sebastien. It was so many years ago. But I do remember a black circle and a big black letter A, upside down in the middle. Almost like, you know ... the anarchy symbol."

A rush of adrenaline surged through my body, and my hands shook as I took my phone out of my jacket packet. I scrolled to Pictures to retrieve the shot I had just taken in the morgue.

"Was it similar to this, Elizabeth?" I asked, showing her the image of the branding between her husband's toes.

"Yes, Sebastien, that's it exactly! This is the same symbol that was on the flag! Where did you get this picture?"

As I gazed at her terrified face, I wished that I did not have to tell her.

Chapter 10

"Buona sera, signore," said the maître d' of Rocco as I entered the restaurant.

"Buona sera," I responded with a smile. *"Come va, Luigi?"* I asked, looking down at the name tag on his black suit. It also stated that he was from Bologna.

He had the typical classy Italian look: hair slicked back with a ton of gel, tanned olive-skinned face, impeccably tailored three-piece suit and a pair of amazing Italian leather shoes. I loved the style; it reminded me of my trip to Italy with Marie. We had visited the Piedmont, where my grandfather came from, but we also went to Venice, Tuscany, Bologna, Rome and Naples. We had a great time, and I always loved to eat true Italian food, not the spaghetti-and-meatball crap served in chain restaurants.

"Va bene, grazie, signore. Parla bene l'italiano," he said.

"Un pochettino. Il mio nonno era di Corneliano d'Alba in Piemonte," I explained, switching to English. "But I am losing it slowly, as I am not practicing enough." I smiled.

"It's better than nothing, sir," he said, also in English, but with a strong accent. Clearly, he was happy to have spoken his native language, even for just a moment, in a city full of foreign tourists. "Do you have a reservation tonight?"

"Yes. I am meeting Ms. Hunter at eight, party of two."

"Very good. Ms. Hunter just arrived a few minutes ago. Please follow me."

Luigi led me to the table, and as I walked behind him he looked over his shoulder. With a big grin on his face, he said, "I recommend the risotto with white truffle. It is succulent. We

51

received a whole pound of it from your grandpa's hometown two days ago."

"*Luigi, sei il migliore!*" I replied. I adored risotto with truffle, so I truly meant it when I said he was the best.

"*Buon appetito, signore e signora,*" he said as we reached the table where Erica sat waiting.

"You look amazing!" I told her. "Still working out and running?"

She stood up, laughing.

I kissed her on both cheeks "So happy to see you!"

"So happy to see you, too!" she said, returning the kiss. "You look pretty good too, I would say. It's good to have you here again in Sin City, capital of money and vice. I hope you're hungry."

"Always!"

We both laughed and then started to talk about our recent races and life in general.

Erica was a terrific woman. I immediately felt at ease in her company, just as I had when we first met. She was not hard to look at, either. Tall—five foot nine, I would say—with a great body. Her dark hair and tanned skin set off gorgeous green eyes. Her smile was very pleasant, showing off perfect white teeth. Some light freckles on her cheekbones gave a sparkle to her beautiful face. She could have been Miss Nevada from my point of view, but I saw her more as Sandra Bullock in the movie *Miss Congeniality,* getting her gun out in the middle of the bikini modeling or kicking butt with some tae kwon do moves. When I asked her why she'd chosen a career in law enforcement, she said it ran in the family. Her dad and grandpa were cops in the small town in Minnesota where she grew up. After graduating from the University of Cincinnati, she moved to Vegas, joined LVMPD, made vice detective and moved up to homicide a few years later. I loved her Midwestern accent and her down-to-earth personality, a trait I admired in most of the

Midwesterners I knew. I also liked the fact that she played sports and stayed active. That was so appealing in a woman. Her last marathon was in Los Angeles at the beginning of the year, and she had finished 514 out of 9,000. She ran it in 3 hours and 22 minutes. My best time was 3 hours and 41 minutes.

After sharing our marathon feats we smiled at each other and then opened our menus.

"What are you in the mood for tonight, Erica?"

"I don't know yet," she said, scanning the menu. "You are part Italian, Seb, what would you suggest?"

"Well, there are many good things here to choose from. The maître d' talked to me about the fresh truffle risotto when I came in. That will be my secondo. For my first course, I'm thinking about doing the antipasto cart. It's beautiful to look at and freshly prepared every day. I am sure you will find something you like there for a starter."

"Yes, antipasto as an appetizer sounds great. I think I'll have the frito misto of vegetables. That sounds very good."

"Great choices. What about starting with two glasses of Prosecco? We can move on to a red after that." I put down my menu and reached for my water glass.

"Sounds like a plan," she responded, flashing her beautiful smile. "I am so happy to have you back in Sin City."

"Thank you. Glad to be back. Too bad it's for such sad business," I said with a shy smile.

"Good evening," said the waiter as he arrived at our table. "Have you made your choices for dinner?" He wore a spotless white shirt, black bowtie, black vest and a clean pressed apron.

"Yes, we have. We will start with your antipasto cart. Then, the lady will have frito misto of vegetables, and I will have the risotto with fresh white truffle. We will start with two glasses of Prosecco, and after the bubblies, we will move on to a 2004 Barolo Sandrone Cannubi Boschis, if you please."

"Very good, sir. Thank you. I will be right back with the sparkling wine."

The light in the restaurant was dimmed pretty low, and music from Andrea Bocelli played in the background. The ambience was that of an upscale trattoria in Northern Italy. Black-and-white photos of people and cities in Italy, dating from the 1960s, filled the walls. I recognized Turin, with the Fiat 500 and the Lingotto car factory; Milano, with La Scala and Piazza del Duomo; and the beautiful coastal towns of Portofino and Santa Margherita. The chairs were comfortable, and the tables were dressed with fine tablecloths and beautiful silverware.

A candle illuminated Erica's tanned face, and she looked astonishingly beautiful in the flame's warm glow, especially her luminous green eyes.

"This place may be too romantic to talk about business, but I just want to talk a little bit about the case, and then we can enjoy our evening. Is that okay with you?" I asked in a soft voice.

"Business before pleasure. Of course. I understand." Her voice was soft too, with a sexy tone.

The server came back with two Riedel glasses filled with Prosecco.

We toasted and then sipped with delight. The wine was nice, and cold enough to kill the flavors. I noticed right away hints of green apple and green grass. It had a great acidity and was a perfect start to a fine meal and a wonderful evening.

Setting down her glass, Erica reached into her bag and pulled out a file with the LVMPD logo on the front. The folder looked brand-new, but it was already an inch thick.

"Are you sure you want to look at the file before eating?" she asked, her tone serious this time.

"I am sure. I need to have an idea of the crime scene. Something is bugging me, but I don't know yet what it is."

Chapter 11

The Handler stopped at a rest area in Silverthorne, Colorado, just a hundred miles from Denver on I-75. He planned to have a quick bite, spend the night and refuel for the rest of his trip. He had a meeting at the Marriott in downtown Denver at ten the following morning, and he wanted to leave early to avoid the morning rush.

He went to the rest area bar and ordered a vegetarian burger, which was absolutely disgusting. It was certainly one of those frozen cheap products that just needed to be defrosted in the microwave, with a minimum of cooking intervention. Some companies were trying to cash in on the vegetarian/vegan fad, but they were doing a terrible job so far.

The man was hungry, so reluctantly he ate his food and drank an iced tea while thinking about his family on the East Coast.

His wife was under the impression that his job was taking him all across the country. She never really did care about what his job actually was, but she most definitely did care when the money reached the bank account. He told her he was a national representative in a new military technology company and that his job required extreme privacy. While at home he could not talk about his job, as it was classified information. In return, his wife never asked him about anything. He was gone all but one week out of every month, and when he did come home it was only to see his son and daughter. He adored his daughter and liked his son very much, but he was starting to really dislike his disengaged wife. He knew she was having an affair with some dad she met in the PTA. He did not care too much about that, as she did play the "good wife" during his monthly appearance, even though she pointedly avoided talking about her daily routines.

The Handler's son and daughter were twins. In September they would start eighth grade; they attended a good middle school in their Washington, DC neighborhood. He tried to spend as much time with them as he could, calling them every two days from wherever he was, just to keep up with their lives. Thankful that the kids seemed to have grown accustomed to his being away from home, he made sure they had no clue as to his real job: hit man for hire.

Pushing the vegetarian burger away in disgust, he pulled out his phone and called his home number to talk to his children. It was 11:00 p.m. on the East Coast, but he needed to talk to them.

"Porter residence. Celeste speaking," said the voice on the other end of the line.

He grinned at the sound of the happy voice.

"Hi, honey, it's Dad. How is my angel tonight?" the Handler asked.

"Hi, Dad! I'm good. How was your Sunday? Not bored yet in Seattle?"

"I'm okay, honey. But yes, I am bored. It rained again today. I went for a walk on Pier 54 and had a horrible coffee. So much for the world-famous coffee here! Aside from that, it's all going okay. I should be home next Sunday."

"Great!" Celeste said, her voice filled with excitement. "I can't wait to see you! You are always away for too long, Dad. I know you have to do it for work, but I wish you could find a job here in DC. The weeks without you take forever! And mom is really getting annoying. She's always on my butt. Damien's too."

"Celeste, it's not easy to raise two kids on your own. I have to give your mom some credit for that. But yes, I am going to try to get a job in DC soon. My job is almost done here, and *the contract will be signed in two weeks. Maybe I'll even take it easy for a little while, stay home and take care of you guys. How would you like that?" The Handler kept his tone light and happy. He knew he was lying through his teeth, but he could not tell them anything about his double life.*

Celeste let out a cry of delight. "I would love that, Dad!"

"Is your mom home tonight?" he finally asked.

The pause in his daughter's excitement revealed her obvious embarrassment. "No, Dad, she went out with some friends to a restaurant. She told us she should be back around midnight."

His daughter was the one truly honest about life, not he.

"That's all right, honey," said the Handler. "How is Damien?"

"He's upstairs on his computer, playing video games. Do you want talk to him?" she asked.

"That's all right, Celeste. Tell your brother I said good night. I'll talk to him next time I call. Listen, you are my angel, and you make me very proud. Keep being my good girl, honey, and remember to be ready to study hard in school this year. It's really important; high school is right around the corner. Love you bunches! Have a great night."

"Love you too, Dad. Say hi to Bill Gates from me," she said, giggling. "Just kidding! Talk to you soon."

The Handler ended the call and put the phone back in his pocket. Talking to his daughter put a grin on his face. He loved her dearly, and she was really the only one he felt bad about lying to. Damien obviously missed having a father figure around, as he was more defiant than Celeste, lashing out at the Handler for being on the road all the time. Damien gave his mother a hard time too, clearly aware that she was far more interested in her social life than in him. Nobody could really blame the kid for that. His wife was distant from the Handler as well, of course, but he did not care about that; he only cared about the effect it had on his children, especially Celeste.

As he was getting ready to pay the bill for his dreadful meal, he made a decision. After completing the job he had now, he would take care of his bitch wife and her PTA boyfriend. He left the bar and headed toward his room for the night, a smile spreading across his face. The Handler already knew how he was going to do it, even if it hurt his children.

Chapter 12

I opened the LVMPD file that Erica passed across the table to me, immediately stunned by the amount of information available. I went through the pages, one by one, in silence.

Erica sat patiently, just watching me and waiting for me to finish reviewing the information.

"That is very meticulous work you have done here, Detective," I told Erica. "I am really impressed." I closed the file, lifted my glass of Prosecco, and toasted with her again. "We are lucky that you were the first one on the scene. Can you tell me a little bit about it as you saw it, please?"

"Well, let's see," she said, pausing for a few seconds. "There's been a flood of information in the past twenty-four hours, Seb, so please bear with me. I want to give you all the info, but I want to make sure it's all accurate." I nodded in understanding, and she continued. "A call came in to 911 at around 10:30 a.m. on Saturday morning, from the cleaning person. She told the 911 operator that she had discovered the body of Chef Bob Dewey on a chair in the kitchen. The operator asked her to see if he was still alive, but she refused, saying she was sure he was dead because he was not moving at all and his eyes were bulging. Dispatch then called homicide, and I answered the phone. I was in between cases, so my boss decided to assign me. We left for the crime scene at about 10:45 a.m., and we got there in fifteen minutes."

"Please describe the crime scene and the feel of the house, Erica. I know we are going there tomorrow, but I want to hear you talk about it," I said slowly.

"It is a beautiful house, in a new suburb of Vegas, in the

northwest corner of the city. The house itself is enormous, Mediterranean architecture, all stone and marble and fountains. The rear of the house backs up to a park. We later found what seemed to be male footprints leading from the park to the house. There was disturbed plant material too. CSI took shots of everything, and they think our intruder weighs around 180 pounds. As we entered the house we were met by the first patrol, which had responded to the call. The maid was being interviewed, and the officer in charge brought us to the kitchen." She paused for a second and then continued. "The scene was really horrible, Seb. It was difficult to recognize the body, as his shirt was taken off, and there were bruises all over the corpse. I quickly looked around the room but did not see any items out of place. It was a gorgeous professional kitchen— perfect for parties, I might add. As I approached the body, I saw that he was barefoot as well. His shoes were laid beside the chair, perfectly parallel to one another. The killer had to have put them there. This showed me right off the bat that we were dealing with an organized personality, someone obsessed with doing meticulous work. We found some traces of blood by the sink, likely the victim's, as our perp does not seem the type to make sloppy mistakes. The chef was shot in the knee, but it was not a critical injury. The killer tried something with a gun, but it did not work for him, for whatever reason. I believe the victim was handcuffed to the chair, and that is where he was tortured. The primary crime scene was the last scene as well."

"Interesting facts. Any sign of forced entry?"

"Yes. The alarm was disabled, and a little window was broken in the living room. No shoe traces, so the killer must have used surgery plastic slip-on shoes. CSI dusted for prints, but there weren't any to be found. The killer wore gloves as well. Again, well organized."

As we were getting deep into the conversation the antipasto cart arrived. The waiter rolled the cart right up to our table. The presentation was splendid, immediately reminding me of my restaurant experiences in Northern Italy, especially Piedmont.

"I am sorry to cut into your conversation, but may I present to you the appetizer cart?" asked the waiter, with a professional smile.

"Go ahead," I said. "We can continue our conversation as we eat."

"Very good, sir. You will find on this cart the typical Northern Italian antipasti. They represent what we call 'appetizers' in the states. Instead of doing just one, though, the Italians give you many choices, so you can taste all of them if you wish." He slowly started to point out all the choices, one by one. "Right here, you have grilled vegetables, served cold, with extra-virgin olive oil. You have zucchini, eggplant, artichoke hearts and red and yellow bell peppers. Right here you will find some fresh anchovies marinated in vinegar; on the right, different types of cured hams and sausage, such as prosciutto di Parma, bresaola, coppa, salame secco, giancale and lardo. Fresh tomato and mozzarella di buffala, with a chiffonade of basil right here. And, finally, a little mix of cheeses, from the softer to the stronger: Tomini in oil; Grana Padano, cousin of the Parmigianino Reggiano; Robiola; Taleggio; and gorgonzola dolce. Plus, you have the choices of homemade breads: grissini di Torino, ciabatta, filone and focaccia."

It seemed an overwhelming amount to choose from, but in Italy you took a little bit of each. I remembered laughing at my mom when she told me to open a trattoria in Omaha, serving this kind of appetizer buffet. I told her people were too used to all-you-can-eat buffets, and they would be upset if we told them they could only get a little bit of each. These antipasti took a long time to prepare. Creating them was an art; they were not just some random frozen products you could throw in the fryer and keep filling the chaffers with. I didn't want people to pile their plates high, mixing those amazing flavors and not appreciating all the work that went into their creation. This Vegas restaurant offered exactly what I remembered from my experiences in Italy—it was no spaghetti-and-meatballs joint!

Erica chose some grilled veggies, some meats and a little cheese. I personally went for the cured meats, which for me represented the best charcuterie a country could offer. I also got some grilled veggies, looking forward to comparing them to my mom's. Last, I selected some anchovies and some cheese. I opted for the ciabatta bread.

Our waiter then brought the Barolo I ordered. He opened the bottle, and I asked him to decant it. Barolos are usually heavier, often requiring some exposure to the air so that they can breathe; the air opens up all the wine's flavors. I smelled it through my right nostril, brought the glass back to the table and swirled it around a few times. I repeated this process, which helped me get an idea of what to expect, not only with the smell, but also with the color and look of the wine. I observed the legs and then I took a sip of the wine in a Spiegelau glass, swirled it in my mouth to coat all the walls, and swallowed. This was great wine. Robert Parker had given it 98 points; *Wine Spectator,* 95 points. It had an aroma of red cherries, with hints of porcini mushroom, licorice, chocolate and fresh Madagascar vanilla. The nose had a "little barn," as we say in wine lingo, but the palate was smooth and rich. I could feel the flavor of raspberry and the aroma of fresh flowers. The wine was perfect, ready to drink, as the tannins were mature and ripe. A real treat!

We started to eat our antipasti but were drawn back to the case in a matter of minutes.

"Was there any blood on the knife you found on the floor, Erica? Did Bob get a chance to defend himself?"

"No. The print on the knife belonged to the chef. I think he got shot before he could do anything with it," she replied.

"It's all over the news now, you know, Seb," she continued. "The Vegas press got it out, and now CNN and other national news outlets all are talking about the murder. They don't know much yet, as I am keeping a lid on it, but I can feel it starting to boil. We have to move fast. I am thinking of giving a press conference in the morning. Any thoughts on that?"

"I think that's a good idea," I said as I was finishing a succulent bite of bagna cauda, roasted bell pepper served with warm garlic, anchovies and oil. "Can you plan it for the afternoon, though? I still want to go to the house in the morning and then back to the morgue to check Bob's body again in detail. I also need to get in contact with a detective in Miami, where Chef Dewey received some threats from some ecoterrorists in 2003."

"All right," Erica said.

"This brings me to an important discovery, Erica. During the autopsy, the ME discovered some burn marks between the toes on the right foot. He did not pay attention to it right away, but after he did some cleaning, he realized this minuscule burn mark appeared to be man-made. After looking at it closely with a magnifying glass, it appeared that Bob had been branded, like they were doing with horses a while ago." I pulled up the photo on my phone and showed it to Erica. "I never saw that symbol in my life. Have you ever seen something like that?" I asked her, with very little hope.

After looking at the image for a few seconds, Erica lifted her eyes from my phone. With a shocked expression on her face, she said, "Yes, I do recognize this logo. If it's who I think it is, Seb, we have a lot of trouble ahead of us."

Chapter 13

"You know this sign, Erica?" I asked, almost dropping the piece of ciabatta I held in my hand.

"Yes. It is the flag of an extremist animal-activist vegan right-wing group based in Colorado. I know that because they have a branch here in Las Vegas, and they have been giving a lot of grief to restaurant owners across the city. Even some casino restaurants protected by the local mafia have been the target of rapid and violent actions. They don't operate legally, but they are getting more and more confident. They have claimed responsibility for many violent acts, just as other eco-terrorist groups do in many other states. They have an official office in a suburb of town, but most of their activists are underground because of the outlawed acts. They pretty much act like the Sinn Fein in Ireland. They try to politicize their cause, and although they claim responsibility for some acts, they blame many of them on unknown groups. I know the FBI is watching them already. Let me call my contact at the bureau now and ask them some questions."

She pulled her iPhone from her purse, dialed, and waited for the agent to pick up the phone. After a few seconds, she mouthed to me that she got voice mail.

"Hi, Gary. It's Erica. Please give me a call ASAP about the Dewey case. We may have a solid lead. Thanks … talk to you later."

"Perfect!" I said, after she put the phone away. I was pleased to have accomplished something concrete with the case. "I'd like to toast to the breakthrough. To Chef Bob Dewey—may we catch his killer soon!"

As I raised my glass, the waiter came to take away our appetizer plates.

We took a break from the case while we waited for the main dishes to arrive. We talked about her life, and I teased her about still being single. She told me she was seeing someone and gave me some background on the guy. I soon realized that her contact at the FBI, Special Agent Gary Duval from the counterterrorism unit, was her "unofficial" boyfriend. I smiled at the news, and she told me they'd just started to date a few months ago.

"It's nothing really serious," she said, watching me to see my reaction.

I avoided her eyes, saved by the arrival of our entrées.

"Risotto con tartufi bianchi di Alba," the waiter said, pronouncing my dish in perfect Italian.

The kitchen and staff had obviously gotten word that a connoisseur of this type of food was in the house tonight. He placed a digital balance to the right of my wineglasses, and next to it, he put a little tray holding a beautiful white truffle. Another waiter brought Erica's dish, which looked beautiful as well, with all its colors.

The maître d', Luigi, then came to the table, weighed the truffle, and said, "The truffle weighs 3.54 ounces, as you can see. We charge by the quarter-ounce. The price is three hundred dollars per ounce. Here is the shaver. Be careful; it is really sharp. Here is a glove to use. Please enjoy. *Buon appetito!"*

As Luigi left us, the waiter took over, making sure we had everything we needed. He described all the different vegetables on Erica's plate and served us more of the Barolo.

I put my glove on, slowly took the shaver, and started to rub the truffle on the blade. A wonderful earthy smell immediately surrounded the table.

Erica stopped eating, inhaling appreciatively as she

watched the perfect shavings fall over my risotto.

I closed my eyes and filled my fork halfway with the creamy risotto and a piece of the shaved truffle. "Enjoy every bite!" I told myself. My teeth went down on the still-warm arborio rice cooked to the perfect texture, and I could feel the fresh truffle break and almost disintegrate on my tongue. Three hundred dollars an ounce, and worth every penny!

"Oh my God! This is amazing," I said.

The flavors were very complex, but I could clearly identify some of them: garlic, cheese and onion, with a hint of the terroir and a pungent smell. Nothing else can compare to the aromas and flavor of this mushroom that can be found under oak trees by pigs and dogs! I understood that some people would never spend the cash for it, and might not even appreciate the delicacy; but I was surely enjoying the moment. Memories brought me back to our family Italian vacation in a little restaurant in the Langue in Northern Italy, where my father had ordered the same dish. It was the first time I saw a real truffle. My dad told me in an almost religious way that the French epicurean Jean Anthelme Brillat-Savarin called these subterranean mushrooms "white diamonds." I've said it before and I'll say it again: expensive but well worth the price!

I was brought back to reality by Erica's laugh. She gazed at me, a big smile spread across her face.

"You look like you're high or in a trance, Seb. Are you sure they didn't serve you some other kind of mushrooms?" She was still puzzled as to how a dish could transport a person to another planet for a few seconds.

"Magical," I said simply. "Please try it!"

I prepared a nice bite of the dish, and she opened her mouth slowly and in a very sexy way, so that I almost poked her with the fork as I was looking into her eyes. She closed her eyes to appreciate the delicacy, and I heard a tiny moan. I guessed she was enjoying it as much as I was!

We continued to talk about things other than business: my ex-wife and my son, the restaurant, and how I was able to manage it all in a twenty-four-hour day. We finished the bottle of Barolo, and I finally asked for the check. I gave them my credit card without even looking at the bill. I knew it was going to be salty, but I did not abuse the white truffle, so I was hoping for a break.

As we were leaving the table and getting our coats, I turned to Erica. "No news from your FBI Gary guy yet?"

"No, not yet," she said. "I will let you know as soon as he calls or texts me. We'll visit the crime scene first thing in the morning, and then I'd like you to come with me to see Gary at the FBI field office, if I can get you in."

"Okay."

"Also, I think it would be wiser to do the press conference later, after we've finished with our investigation for the day. We might find more evidence and information." When I nodded in agreement, she continued. "I will ask my boss to set it up for 7:00 p.m. at LVMPD headquarters."

"Sounds good," I said.

She looked straight into my eyes. "I had a great evening, Seb. There's nothing better than talking about work and personal life at the same time. I loved it. Thank you very much for dinner."

"You are very welcome," I said as I gave her a hug.

Man! She was beautiful. But I stopped myself from saying anything out of place. Instead, I gave her a big kiss on each of her warm cheeks. She smelled of fresh vegetables and perfume. I felt a rush to ask her for another drink but changed my mind. Tomorrow was going to be another busy day, and I still wanted to do some research on the web about that animal-rights activist group.

We parted, saying good-bye for the fifth time, as if we did not want to separate, and then we agreed to meet at Chef

Dewey's house at 8:00 a.m.

I walked to my car on the third level of the parking garage, after passing what seemed like a mile of casinos and shops. The air was still very warm and dry, and the Barolo was having a happy effect on me. As I approached my rental car, I heard the squeal of car tires behind me. I turned around, and in a split second saw a black sedan with its lights on coming directly at me. In a quick desperate move, I jumped behind a red jeep parked right by me, and got my gun out. I hit the pavement hard, as I was not ready for the landing, got up feeling pain in my right shoulder, and aimed at the runaway car. The vehicle was going very fast, and I could see some other people watching the action as they stood beside their cars in the parking garage, so I decided to not take a shot, afraid that I might hit someone. I tried to get the license plate, but I could only get a partial read because the car was moving so fast. All I could see were the numbers 1 and 5 at the beginning, and B or S or 8 at the end. The plates were dirty and dusty. I started to run in the direction of the exit, yelling at people to move away, as I was hoping to get a glance at the driver. But it was too little, too late. The sedan picked up speed and disappeared into the busy street.

Swearing and trying to catch my breath, I pulled my phone out and called Erica.

"Erica! Someone just tried to run me over. A dark Ford sedan, with the partial license plate 1-5, and maybe a B or S or 8 at the end. It escaped, headed south on South Las Vegas Boulevard. Please call it in right away!"

"I will," she said. "Are you okay, Seb? Do you need me to come back?"

I heard a little panic in her voice. "No, I'm all right," I told her. "Please keep me updated if you find them. Otherwise, I'll see you tomorrow morning at eight, at Chef Dewey's house."

I put the phone back in my pocket, muttering to myself,

"Damn it! What in the world is going on? How do they know about me being here?"

Chapter 14

I must have fallen asleep pretty fast last night. I woke up at around 6:00 a.m. with a splitting headache. This was not from the wine, to be sure, but from my dive last night in the parking lot, followed by an hour-long explanation to casino security and the LVMPD. The headache had started by the time I got back to the hotel. I took some aspirin to try to get rid of it, but obviously, that did not work. Groaning into the pillow, I forced myself out of bed.

After making coffee in the room, I went down to the gym and ran a quick four miles on the treadmill. The TV was on in the gym, tuned to CNN, which didn't report anything new on the case. Apparently it was old news for them, as they had turned their attention to some church sex-abuse scandal on the East Coast. I used the remote to switch to the local news, which gave some information on the case, including some details about Chef Bob Dewey. The man was adored by the media and the public. They talked about the different charities he had supported, the cooking shows he'd been on, and the businesses he had been a part of. He'd been a busy man with a full life, and he had clearly loved his work. He was one of the last famous chefs to still work the line in his restaurants, and everything indicated that he'd adored doing it. The report included a brief mention of Chef Patsy Williams, who now owned La Cigale in Omaha, and Master Chef Pierre LeJeune, who now owned Celadon in Chicago. All three chefs had starred in a show on the Food Network, *True Food Origin,* and they'd co-owned a restaurant, Above the Stars, in the King Arthur Hotel and Casino in Vegas. The show had gone off the air many years ago, and the restaurant venture had been a long time ago as well. I had known about the show, but I hadn't heard of the restaurant until Elizabeth mentioned it briefly when I spoke with her in the coroner's office, and she hadn't indicated that Bob had co-owned the place with the other two chefs, his Food Network co-stars. According to the report, the King Arthur was brand-new when Above the Stars opened, and along with Fantasy Land, it was considered the "child friendly" spot on the Strip at that time.

I reminded myself that I needed to call Patsy to keep her updated, as I'd promised her I would do.

After taking a quick shower and getting dressed, I stopped for a bite to eat in the lobby of the hotel, and then I headed to Chef Dewey's house. It was a five-minute ride from the hotel to the house, but I found myself in the midst of the morning rush hour. This traffic jam was quite different from the one I'd encountered last night on the Strip, where all the cars were driven by tourists. This morning I was surrounded by people who actually worked normal hours, much like I encountered every morning at home in Omaha. The morning sun was very bright in Vegas—not helping my head too much!—and so the town looked quite different than it did at night, with neon signs and bright lights glaring everywhere. It seemed almost surreal.

I found the development, and actually arrived at the house on time. Erica's car was already parked in front, with an LVMPD cruiser right behind it. The enormous house dwarfed both vehicles. I steered my rental into the driveway, parked, and got out. An officer immediately came over to me and I took out my badge and introduced myself, telling him that Detective Hunter expected me.

"She's inside, Detective," said the officer. "Go right in."

"Good morning, Seb. Rough night last night?" Erica asked with a smile as she stepped into the front doorway, holding the door open for me.

"Yes, it was," I responded, gesturing toward my injured shoulder. "No luck on the runaway car, I assume?"

"No luck so far, but we still have an APB out. They are running the plates at the squad as we speak. It could be a stolen vehicle, so we might get lucky later today."

I nodded.

"Come on in," she said. "I'll show you the crime scene and the rest of the property."

We walked the whole house and the backyard. She showed me the different breached entrance points throughout the property, saving the kitchen for last.

Finally, I saw the site where murder occurred during the wee hours of Saturday morning. The chair where Chef Dewey had been tortured was moved to the side. Brushes and dust for fingerprinting were everywhere, but Erica said that the killer had not left any clues except his calling card: the branding mark between the victim's toes. I was at a loss at this point. I'd wanted to see the scene for myself, but no clues jumped out at me. Erica had been over it all with a fine-tooth comb already, so she didn't see anything new. CSI had taken numerous photos of the kitchen; we had enough of them to re-create the whole kitchen in the lab, if need be.

"They are going to release the body to Elizabeth today," I told Erica. "She's bringing him back to New York for burial. Her two kids got here last night, so they're helping her. It's good. I'll call her and let her know what's going on."

"That's fine, Seb," Erica said. "I have news from the FBI. I spoke with Gary last night after your incident. I did not want to bother you after that, but he did have quite a bit of info. He was not surprised by our findings. He asked me to come for a debriefing on the eco-terrorist groups operating here in Nevada, as well as other parts of the US. I asked if you could come, and he said yes. It looks like the bureau may have some information that we don't have, and they're ready to share."

"Great!" I responded.

"The debriefing is at ten, so we need to get moving."

"Okay," I said. "Can I ride with you? I can drop my car at the hotel, and then we can head to the FBI field office together."

"No problem. I will meet you at the hotel in a few minutes."

At 9:45 a.m. we were on our way to see Special Agent Gary Duval, the man in charge of the counterterrorism unit for the state of Nevada.

I pulled my phone out to make two important calls. First I called Elizabeth, so I could update her on all that we had uncovered.

"I promise to keep you in the loop, Elizabeth," I said, after I had recapped the investigation thus far.

"Thank you, Sebastien," she said. "The kids and I have an afternoon flight today. The funeral will be on Saturday. I'll call you with the details."

I ended the call and dialed Patsy in Omaha. It had to be close to opening time at the restaurant, but I knew she would not mind. I was keeping my promise to let her know what I found out about Bob's murder.

A friendly female voice answered the phone. "La Cigale. This is Jenny. May I help you?"

"Hi, Jenny. This is Chef Sebastien Saint-Gemmes from the Drunken Frog. I know you are getting ready to open, but may I speak to Patsy, please? She is expecting my call."

"Absolutely," she said. "Please hold for a moment."

"Thank you."

Jenny put me on hold, and I listened to the great voice of Charles Aznavour while I waited for Patsy to pick up.

"Hi, Seb," Patsy said. "How are you doing? Any news on this horrible incident?"

I could hear a door shut, so I knew she was closing herself in her office.

"Well, yes and no. We have a lead on an eco-terrorist group through the FBI. I will know more after I meet with them."

"That sounds like a good lead."

"I hope so. Time will tell. By the way, I heard your name on the news this morning while I was in the gym. I knew you lived in Vegas before, but I did not know you had a restaurant with Chef Dewey and Master Chef LeJeune."

"Oh yes, a long time ago. We had a great spot in the King Arthur when it opened, a year or so after our three-year stint on the Food Network. All this was twenty-odd years ago Seb. We called the restaurant Above the Stars, and it was a huge success with kids. That was just at the time when Vegas started to become a family destination. We did very well for five years or so, and then an incident caused us to close the restaurant. Bad case of food poisoning."

"Interesting," I said distractedly. My mind raced through a million details as I spoke to her. "I will need to talk to you more about that when I come back to Omaha."

"No problem Seb. Just let me know when. Keep me updated on your search, please."

"I will."

"When is Bob's funeral?"

"It will be on Saturday, in New York. Elizabeth will give me details later, and I will send you the info.

We said good-bye.

As I put my phone back in my pocket, Erica pulled the car up to the gates of the FBI compound, showing her credentials to the armed guard.

Chapter 15

The Handler entered the Marriott in downtown Denver at exactly 9:45 a.m., fifteen minutes ahead of his scheduled appointment time. He always arrived early for his appointments. "Arriving first shows your superiority over the latecomer, even if he is on time. Always be first!" his dad had always said. The Handler could recall that he was only seven years old the first time his dad told him this. At the time, he would have far preferred to go play with his friends instead of receiving civility lessons from his father. But today he was happy he had learned those lessons at a young age. He tried to educate his kids the same way, but it was more difficult. He smiled, thinking about Celeste; his daughter seemed to be the only one who cared about what he had to say. "My loving angel," he said aloud softly.

He was supposed to register at the desk, go up to the room, and wait for instructions.

"Robert Smith," he said to the desk clerk. "I have a reservation for one night. Do you have a room ready for me?" He always chose the most basic names, ones that would not attract any attention. He would have preferred to use Umberto Eco or James Patterson, just for fun, but unfortunately, this was no fun game he was playing.

"Yes, Mr. Smith," said the clerk. "I have a room for you ready on level 6: room 665. Can I see a photo ID and a credit card, please? It's just for identification; we are not charging the room on this card," she added with a professional smile.

"That's all right. It's my company card. I'll use it to pay the final bill," he said as he pulled out the forged Washington

State ID, complete with his photo, the name Robert Smith and a Seattle address. He then handed her a credit card bearing the name Robert Smith as well.

While the clerk checked him in, he recalled the day he'd received the package containing all his identification for this job. UPS had delivered it to his house in DC, and he'd carefully checked all the contents behind closed doors in his home office. There was the fake Washington State ID, a fake US passport, and two credit cards—all of them under the phony name. There was also ten thousand dollars in cash in an envelope, along with a note from his new boss. The note indicated that each card had a credit limit of fifty thousand dollars, and that more would come when the job was accomplished. There was also a list of the code names of his three targets. He had a year to prepare his hits before he would be given the victims' real names and other particulars.

Today was the day he would learn about his most important objective: the final one that would earn him the prize of two million dollars. Money did not seem to be a problem for his employer. This one just wanted results, and good ones. The Handler did not feel threatened, but he knew it was better to follow orders and not diverge from the plan. His boss knew about his personal life and family. So far, the arrangement had been great for the Handler: one target down, two more to go. By the end of the week he would be done here, and then he would fly to the destination his boss chose so that he could get his prize.

"Enjoy your stay, sir," said the clerk as she handed him the key card for the room.

The Handler took it, crossed the lobby to the elevator and went up to the sixth floor. The hotel seemed to have been recently renovated, as the smell of new carpet assailed his nostrils when he opened the door to his room. He stepped inside, looked around and dropped his bag on the floor. He looked at his watch: 9:55 a.m. He sat down at the desk and admired the beautiful view of downtown Denver, with the mountains in the distance, soaring above the horizon.

Suddenly, he heard a tap on the door. He turned around, pulled out his gun and slowly walked toward the entrance. Looking down, he saw that an envelope had been slipped under the door. He slowly picked it up and backed away from the door. He opened the envelope and pulled out the contents: a simple piece of paper with three pictures on it. He looked at the paper and immediately recognized Chef Bob Dewey and the two other targets. There was a large X through Chef Dewey's face. This meant his boss acknowledged his accomplishment of eliminating the first target.

For an instant, he wondered why all this was happening. But then, just as quickly, he told himself it did not matter. He was a gun for hire. All he knew now was that he had two more targets to eliminate in order to complete this job in the states, and then he would be using that passport.

It would not be long before he could collect his prize.

Chapter 16

"Special Agent Gary Duval," said the tall, well-built man who greeted us. "Nice to meet you, Detective Saint-Gemmes."

He and I shook hands, and then he ushered Erica and me into the conference room of the FBI field office.

As the man in charge of the FBI's counterterrorism unit in Las Vegas, Agent Duval was certainly a busy man. I appreciated his taking the time to read us in on the different ecoterrorism activities going on in Las Vegas and its environs.

"Good to meet you too," I said. "Thank you for receiving us on such short notice."

He smiled, looking at Erica, and his expression said, "Don't thank me. Thank Erica."

"Yes, Agent Duval, I appreciate your agreeing to take time to read us in, too," Erica said quickly. "It will really help us with our investigation."

"Happy to help," Agent Duval said.

"You said you might have information on some eco-terrorist groups acting in the region, especially Vegas," Erica said, prompting Agent Duval to take the lead on the meeting.

"I did, and we do," he said. "Please have a seat. I've prepared a quick summary of the different groups and their leaders. We have the groups separated by their causes and the levels of extremism they each show. A minority of them can be very dangerous, and some groups have actually committed crimes. The majority of them are just trying to ensure fair treatment of animals. Not everybody will agree with the actions of these animal lovers, and some of them do have a strange way of fighting for their cause, but most are not crazy enough to commit a felony."

He switched on the large-screen TV in front of us, and then he opened the laptop sitting on the large oval table emblazoned with a huge FBI crest. Turning toward Erica and me he asked, "Can I get you coffee, tea, water?"

Erica and I both declined.

"Okay," he said. "Let's get started."

I looked around the room while Agent Duval's presentation loaded. The walls bore framed photos of the President of the United States and the Director of the Federal Bureau of Investigation, respectively. On another wall there were two dozen or so clocks, each one showing the current time in a different place in the world. I searched for the one with the Paris time: 7:12 p.m. I tried to imagine what the members of my extended family still living in Paris were doing at the moment.

The PowerPoint presentation loaded on the TV screen and Agent Duval began speaking.

"To pick up on what I was saying earlier, we have to make the distinction between two groups here. The first group is comprised of all the ecoterrorists, and the second group is made up of all the animal-rights activists. Both are extremist groups, and together we consider them to represent the most serious domestic terrorist threat in the country today. Since the FBI started to keep track of them in 1979 they have collectively committed more than two thousand crimes. Their actions have had significant economic impact, with financial losses in excess of $110 million dollars. Again, that's a collective figure representing the actions of all the groups combined." He paused to take a breath but kept the presentation going. "A lot of different companies and people are the victims of the acts of these groups. They've hit lumber companies, international corporations, animal-testing facilities, genetic-research firms, fisheries and so on; even some restaurant chefs have been the victims of personal attacks. The violent rhetoric and tactics of these groups keep getting bolder. In fact, not too long ago this office received a letter that had been sent to a California product-testing company, which read, "You might be able to protect your buildings, but can you protect the home of every employee?'."

Erica and I looked at each other, and then we both looked at Agent Duval.

"Yeah, it's very intense stuff. The people we are dealing with here are sociopaths," he said.

I wanted to hear more about the chefs who had been personally targeted, but Erica shot me a look, so I kept my mouth shut, letting Special Agent Gary Duval run his show, his way.

Agent Duval continued. "The two most dangerous groups today are the Animal Liberation Front and the Earth Liberation Front, also known by their respective acronyms: ALF and ELF. ALF was created in England in 1976, by a man named Ronnie Lee; it's still active in more than forty countries. The US is high on ALF's radar, because the group is very active against pharmaceutical companies. These guys are most interested in protecting animals of any kind. ELF, on the other hand, focuses more on nature in general; its fight is to protect and preserve the environment. ELF was also created in England, but not until 1992. It is now an international movement present in seventeen countries, and we regard it as having arisen from ALF. Both groups have similar guidelines and tactics, such as fire bombings, assaults, stalking, arson, vandalism, intimidation and so on. ELF will burn brand-new resorts in the mountains, and ALF will resort to violence against those who keep so-called free animals in cages. For example, our Los Angeles field office worked on the case of Chef Florent Riqueman in San Francisco, when his restaurant and home were destroyed because he was selling foie gras. Activists held him hostage for a few hours and terrorized his family. He left the Bay Area after that, moving to

Louisiana. A favorite quote of both groups is: 'Economic sabotage and guerrilla warfare to stop the exploitation and destruction of the environment.' That said, ALF and/or one of its subgroups may have killed Chef Bob Dewey, so the FBI has decided to open an investigation, in coordination with the LVMPD, to track the murderer."

So that was the real reason Agent Duval had been so forthcoming with his offer of assistance. Well, that plus his personal interest in Erica. But who knew which took precedence over the other? I did not like where this was going one bit.

I tried to catch Erica's attention, but she avoided eye contact.

"Before you say anything, let me show you the different factions affiliated with, or close to, ALF," Special Agent Gary Duval said quickly. He started to go through slides of different factions, their alleged leaders and lieutenants, their addresses, mottos, logos, etc.

It looked like a lot of them were very active, spread all around the US. Different ones caught my eye, such as the one located in Norfolk, Nebraska, and a few others not too far from Omaha. Suddenly, the flag with the upside-down A came on the screen.

"Stop right there, please, Agent Duval," I said. "That is the logo of the group that seems to be involved in the murder." I took out my phone and showed him the photo of the branding mark between Chef Dewey's toes, explaining what I had learned from Dr. Saravoh.

Erica interjected with a quick recap of the incident in the Palm Grove Resort and Casino parking lot the night before, finishing with, "There's an APB out on the car, but we don't yet know the identity of the perp."

"This is really good information and clues," Agent Duval said. "Now let's get into the details on this organization."

As he smiled, I thought to myself that this was the first

genuine reaction I'd seen from the man.

It seemed we were going to be in the conference room for a while, so I settled more comfortably in the leather chair. Turning to face Erica, I said, "We should have a pretty good profile for the press conference."

"I agree. I'm going to call my boss to ask him to set it up for 7:00 p.m., like you and I discussed. We have a lot of work to do before then, so we'd better get to it." Turning to Agent Duval, she said, "I know it's early, but I'm starving. Can we order sandwiches or pizza?"

"Sure. There's a great pizzeria a block away, and they prepare very unusual pies, not the pepperoni-and-cheese standard."

"Sounds like my type of pizza," I said with a smile on my face.

Erica laughed, but Agent Duval offered no response. Wordlessly, he switched the TV to the Internet, typed the name of the pizza place and clicked on the menu.

It was perfect! This was no pizza chain. This was exactly the style of pizza I would offer if I owned a pizzeria in Omaha. All the choices covered a wide array of ingredients typical of a fine restaurant. In this case, they were arranged on a beautiful piece of dough baked in a wood-fired oven. The menus said they used only 00 grade Italian flour, which had a greater amount of ash and less gluten. The wood gave the pizza the beautiful smoked and burned flavors associated with pizzerias in Italy.

We each ordered a personal-size pizza. I opted for the one with crème fraîche, roasted fingerling potatoes, duck confit, herbs de Provence, shallots and a sprinkle of Gruyère cheese. Erica again went for the roasted vegetables: grilled zucchini, grilled eggplant and roasted bell peppers, all on a bed of garlic hummus atop the crust. Agent Duval decided on slow-roasted pork shoulder with homemade barbecue sauce, topped with mushrooms.

I pushed myself out of chef mode, even though my mouth was watering for my pizza, and stayed focused on my task as a detective. It was extremely difficult to manage the duality of my existence when food was involved, especially when I was hungry. At such moments I was definitely a gourmand first—or should I say foodie—and a detective second!

We continued to talk about the case as we waited for our pizzas to be delivered.

"The group whose logo Detective Saint-Gemmes identified is called Vegan National," Agent Duval said. "Its ringleader is named Daryl Parker. He's forty-seven years old and originally from Portland, Oregon. Parker's father was a farmer who raised cows for milk consumption, cheese making and then meat production. He took off early on, and Parker's mother went to work at a meat factory to support herself and her son. Parker then attended the University of Oregon, where he first encountered animal-rights activists. He started with ALF but quickly broke ranks, deciding to create his own action group. That's how Vegan National started. He did not stay in Oregon too long after that; he quit the university and moved to Colorado. We don't know exactly where he is at this moment, but he is a wanted man, for both arson and murder. His first criminal act happened in San Bernardino, California, where he burned down an entire building. The company that owned the building was doing medical research on cats, dogs and monkeys. Parker and his people freed all the animals, and then they started the fire. A guard died while trying to put out the blaze. I don't think it was Parker's goal to kill anyone in this case, but it did happen. He went underground after that, and he must have the right connections, because he is still on the loose today and commanding more terrorist actions. Their headquarters location is in Denver, but they have satellite offices in twenty states. James Tobert is the official face of the group. You should pay a visit to their local branch here in Vegas. A bunch of stoned hooligans, if you ask me; their sole purpose is to annoy and destroy people. The lead contact here in Vegas is Germaine Logan. They are located in the suburb of Southeast Vegas, on Green Valley Road." He wrote down the address on a piece of paper and gave it to Erica. "The FBI is trying hard to find where the money to finance those operations comes from. We are thinking about doing a raid of all of the Vegan National offices in the US."

A knock on the door broke our concentration, and a junior intern brought in our pizza.

"Fresh pizza in!" he said with a hungry smile on his face.

My own stomach growled.

"Thank you, Brian," Agent Duval said. "Close the door behind you, please." It was obvious he was annoyed to have been stopped fast in his tracks. "Well, let's just eat as I continue the presentation. I should be done in five minutes."

We ate our delicious pizza while listening to more information about Vegan National.

The presentation grew more and more monotonous. As the flavors of the ingredients, enhanced by the wood smoke, excited my taste buds, I started to think about what our next move should be.

Agent Duval stated that he would lead some agents in the process of obtaining information about the group.

I wanted to be in their company, but I would wait for him to offer that opportunity. Again, I thought about the Sinn Fein correlation, wondering what we could expect to see and find there. I also wanted to talk to the staff at Tartufo to see if they had had ideas or clues about who could have tortured and murdered their boss. Perhaps that should be my venue for dinner. Once again, food came first.

Erica's phone rang, interrupting my thoughts.

Excusing herself, she got up and stepped away from the table. "Detective Hunter speaking," she said, turning to look at Agent Duval and me. "That's great news! We're on our way right now."

Putting her phone away she grabbed her jacket. "That was dispatch," she said. "A patrol spotted the vehicle from last night. Guess where?"

In an instant I was right behind her, and we raced out the door.

Chapter 17

Erica put the siren on in the car so we could reach our destination faster. During our trip she called her boss to ask him to deploy a SWAT team to assist us, and also to schedule the press conference for 7:00 p.m.

She hoped, as I did, that we would gather some great information at Vegan National's office. Whatever we found we would need to act on quickly. This was the only solid lead we had at the moment. In addition, based on Agent Duval's presentation, Erica and I both understood that ecoterrorism was a big part of the potential threats to our country and our economy. It was a different kind of terrorism than the Oklahoma City bombing—or 9/11 for that matter. Those threats needed to be addressed immediately, and everyone in law enforcement fought hard to prevent such acts from occurring—and to restore order and rescue victims when prevention did not work. Ecoterrorism was something else entirely. And the big payoff it promised its proponents made it difficult to believe there was any honor in their intentions to serve their so-called noble cause.

Erica ended her call. "Good news, Seb," she said to me, her voice raised so I could hear her above the blare of the siren. "My boss agrees with us. He's going to get back to me about the time for the press conference. Hopefully, we'll get some concrete proof on the murder case while we go in on the vehicle. Backup units are on the way. A car fitting the description you gave, with a similar license plate, was seen in an alley a block away from the Vegan National office. It's definitely our car."

I agreed.

A few minutes later we arrived at the address and two patrol cars were already there, parked in a protective V angle at the front of the office, with their lights on, blocking all access to and from the street. The local branch was a stand-alone building located in a deserted area of town where most of the shops had boarded doors and windows. Trash and debris were laying on the sidewalk and the street. The atmosphere surrounding the place looked almost surreal. The blinds were down and a "closed" sign was on the door. The place looked totally dead.

Two of the officers were standing behind their car waiting for us.

As I was way out of my jurisdiction, there was a limit to what I could and could not do. I had to take the lead from Erica.

We got out of the car and went straight to the trunk. Erica took out an extra bulletproof vest and an earpiece radio system, handing them to me.

When I looked inside the trunk I saw that it was loaded with heavy weaponry. "Wow!" I said. "That is a pretty impressive arsenal."

She turned, gave me a sexy smile, and winked.

"Women and guns, the perfect combination for me," I said as I put on the LVMPD vest and affixed the earpiece.

"Remember, Seb, you're here as a spectator, not an actor."

"Yes, ma'am," I said.

Erica had already made it very clear that she was responsible for me in Las Vegas. She knew I understood that.

We nodded to each other and then joined the other units.

"The door is locked, Detective, but we saw some movements inside," one of the LVMPD officers told Erica.

"SWAT is on the way. Did you check the back door or alley?" Erica asked as she pulled out her revolver.

"Yes, ma'am. Sergeant Mahoney and Officer Delco are behind the house. I am in contact with them right now. They're on channel 32 if you want to talk to them."

"Sergeant, this is Detective Hunter from homicide. Do not try anything. The SWAT team is on the way right now. They will handle the entrance and the search. We are dealing with potential terrorists."

"I see someone with a shotgun. He's right by the window. I hear them yelling. It doesn't look good." His voice sounded frantic.

"Stand down, Sergeant," Erica said calmly. "They can't go anywhere. The office is surrounded and—"

With that, shots rang out in the back of the building, and voices scrambled on the audio.

"Officer down! Officer down!" Officer Delco yelled on the radio. "I am hit as well."

"Delco, stay with me," Erica said.

Officer Delco groaned over the radio.

Addressing the other LVMPD officers with us, Erica said, "You two, stay put. Secure the front door. Nobody is getting out of here. Call for more reinforcement, now, and an ambulance!" Turning toward me, she said, "Seb, let's go in the back. Catch this!"

She tossed me a Remington Law Enforcement 11-87 semiautomatic shotgun, and I caught it.

"I am the lead," she reiterated. "Just watch my back, and shoot only if you have to."

"Yes ma'am," I said again. My heart was pumping. The adrenaline rush was what made the job so enjoyable and exciting. It was the same thing I loved about the incredible pace I had to maintain when cooking, working the line at the restaurant on a Saturday night—on a different level, of course. In both cases, there were so many things happening at once, and you had to focus on all of them, which you could only do by keeping a cool head and concentrating on the task.

I followed Erica along the wall in the back alley on the right side of the one-story building. She was running fast, with her .45 clasped in both hands. I was right behind her, with my hand on the safety of the shotgun, ready to act if needed. Erica stopped at the corner of the building, and with a quick movement of her head, looked in the back.

"Two men down, right there," she said quietly. "I'm going to the garbage bin over there," she added as she pointed at it. "Then I'll cover you. Ready, go—"

"Wait!" I shouted, interrupting her.

But it was too late. She was already running through the courtyard just as a shot rang out. I saw her fall behind the bin.

"Damn it!" I said between my teeth. "Erica, can you hear me?"

I didn't see her move at first, but I knew she was hit. I could see some blood starting to stain her left sleeve. I hoped it wouldn't be serious.

"Third officer down!" I said on my radio. "We need backup, now!"

At that moment I saw a young male and female sprint across the yard, headed in the direction of the back alley. The male suspect, who seemed to be in his twenties, had dark hair and was about five foot ten. He carried a shotgun. The young lady also looked to be in her twenties. She was blonde, wore jeans full of holes and carried a pistol. From their actions it looked like they didn't care if they got shot; they were trying to make a run for it and were not going to stop.

"Police!" I shouted, kneeling down on the ground. "Stay where you are! Drop your weapons!"

They didn't even seem to hear me. They continued to run, the dust flying in the air behind them. As they passed the garbage bin Erica swiftly extended her right leg, and the young lady fell facedown, losing her gun.

I started to run at that moment, not really paying attention to whether a third suspect was behind me. All I knew was that Erica was in no physical shape to take on an armed person. With the bottom of my shotgun, I smashed the young lady's hand as she inched closer to retrieve her dropped weapon. She moaned in pain, and I kicked her weapon out of reach as I put Erica's handcuffs on her.

"Are you okay for now?" I asked Erica as I tightened up the bracelets on our suspect, keeping an eye on her accomplice as he continued to run.

"I'm good; shot in the left arm. I'll survive," she said. "Seb, go get him! I'll watch her." Erica was now standing next to me with her gun in her hand. "Go!"

The girl still lay face down in the dirt.

I left the shotgun with Erica, as it was too heavy to carry for a foot chase.

Taking out my OPD service revolver, I started to run in the direction of the young guy. The heat of the day was at its peak, and I could feel some sweat starting to form on my chest. I tried right away to find the breathing rhythm I was used to when running a race. With my free hand I put my OPD badge around my neck so I would not look like a madman racing through the streets, brandishing a gun. I did not want to shoot the gun, as a lot of paperwork was required afterward to explain why the weapon had been discharged. I just hoped to catch the guy soon, and, if possible, not to have to injure him.

Suddenly, out of the corner of my eye, I saw the young man, but I didn't see the weapon in his hand. "He must have dropped it somewhere," I thought to myself. "Be careful, he may be hiding it."

"Police! Stop where you are, right now!" I yelled as I caught up with him.

He looked back at me with a scared face, and with no time to spare, I took a swing at his legs as he kept running.

Bingo! Uttering a few curses, he went down hard on the pavement, face-first. I stopped, standing over him and pumping my gun. When he turned his head to look at me, I pointed the gun at his bloody face.

"I wish I had killed you yesterday, motherfucker," he said with a grin on his face.

Chapter 18

As I was bringing in my suspect, I saw that Special Agent Gary Duval had arrived on the scene, along with other FBI agents from the counterterrorism unit and a team from the Department of Homeland Security. Two DHS agents dressed in assault gear took the suspect away from me.

Flashing blue and red lights were everywhere: fire trucks, ambulances, sheriff's department cars and LVMPD cruisers.

An EMT was tending to Erica, applying first aid to her injured arm. I walked toward where she sat on the open tailgate of the ambulance.

"She'll be fine," the paramedic told me. "We're going to take her to the hospital, just as a precaution."

"You're very lucky Erica," I said, relieved. "Please don't run away like that again without telling me first."

"I know I should have told you before I did it," she said sheepishly, sticking out her tongue at me. "But in the heat of the moment, I just … anyway, the good news is that I only have a few BBs in my arm. I just need some bandages and clearance from a doctor, and then I can be back on the job. Here are my keys, Seb. Come and get me in an hour. I'll be at the Valley Hospital Medical Center. *Ple-e-e-ase!*" She turned toward me, with the look of a sad puppy, and rose from the ambulance tailgate.

"I will," I told her, kissing her forehead as I took her keys. "I'm going to stay here and check on things. See you later."

I turned in the direction of the only other person I knew

in the crowd: Special Agent Gary Duval.

He was looking at the exiting ambulance, and then he turned to address me. "What exactly happened, Saint-Gemmes? How come I have three officers shot? The situation looks pretty serious right now. The FBI and DHS are entering all the Vegan National offices in the US as we speak. We have three officers injured, one seriously, and two punk heads in custody. Talk to me."

"Well, it seemed like they were waiting for us. I need to talk to the male suspect. He tried to run me over last night, and I need to know why, and also what he knows about the murder of Chef Bob Dewey. I'm pretty sure everything is tangled together."

"The counterterrorism unit is taking them into custody at our FBI field office. We need everybody to be debriefed in the next twenty-four hours. When are you leaving town?" he asked me as we walked toward the building.

"I have a flight tomorrow afternoon."

"Great," he said. "I'd like to have a debriefing at field HQ tomorrow. I'm planning on 8:00 a.m., but Quantico needs to approve. Please join us; all the interested parties will be there. I'll confirm the time with Erica. We need to go through the paperwork inside the office now."

A SWAT team had secured the building, and then a team of specialists had done a more meticulous sweep of the building, checking the doors, lighting system, etc., to make sure that nothing was booby-trapped.

We entered the building. People in dark suits and uniforms were hard at work, taking photos from every angle and putting papers in boxes. Some FBI agents were taking computers and hard drives and bringing them to a central truck parked out front.

"Special Agent Duval, please come over here!" a voice came out of the room located near the main entrance.

We entered a dark room without any windows where the smell of enclosed trash, coffee and putrefied banana assailed our nostrils immediately.

A DHS agent named John Casper nodded to us. He was a very tall, skinny man, wearing a dark suit covered with a jacket labeled DHS on the back. He introduced himself to me, and we shook hands. He and Agent Duval greeted each other.

Agent Casper said, "We are dealing with a very important network of ecoterrorism, as you can see."

To my surprise, all the walls of the room were covered with pictures, maps, newspaper articles and handwritten notes. Stacks of papers were still on the table in the middle of the room, and two other men were already going through them. The scene was like something you would see in a movie. But this was real, and it was definitely getting serious on the national level. I looked around the room, and two maps of the United States caught my eye.

One of the maps had around twenty green dots dispersed all over it, mostly in midsize to large western cities: Spokane, Seattle and Tacoma in Washington State; Portland, Eugene, Coos Bay and Salem in Oregon; Billings and Great Falls in Montana; Boise in Idaho; Reno and Las Vegas in Nevada; and plenty more in California. The dots did not go farther east of Chicago, Illinois (to the north) and New Orleans, Louisiana (to the south). Could all those dots represent offices of Vegan National?

The second map had red dots; more than the green ones, maybe thirty to forty. These dots were scattered all over the US. I looked at the state of Nebraska, as a reflex action, and was stunned to see two red dots in the city of Omaha.

With a nervous smile I said, "I guess we are getting to be a big red state."

"Looks like it," Special Agent Duval said, from the other side of the room. "I knew you owned a restaurant, Detective

Saint-Gemmes, but I did not know you were a well-known culinarian," he added. "Come and see."

I turned around to look at him where he stood, going through newspaper clips. As I approached him the board caught my attention, and I noticed what looked like a complex system of strings with wrapped tacks connecting articles to pictures. He pointed to a set of images, and I stopped straightaway.

"What in the world is going on?" I said as a chill shot up my spine.

In front of me was a photo of Chef Patsy Williams and me, cooking at La Cigale. That same Sunday meal I had long cherished and recalled with such fondness suddenly filled me with dread.

Chapter 19

After spending more than an hour going over additional papers and maps, I got a clear idea of the identities of Vegan National's targets. All were individuals who worked in the food service industry. Many were chefs and independent restaurateurs, others were CEOs of restaurant groups and franchises, executives of the National Restaurant Association, Food Network celebrities and so on. Even food growers and producers were part of the giant plan of action. Some of the targets were named, and descriptions of their companies, headquarters, and production plants were also listed. The scariest part was that Vegan National had the names and addresses of the family members of the targeted individuals. It had taken a lot of research to get all that information. I noticed ConAgra, in Omaha, as well as a few other companies that Moose and I worked with at the Drunken Frog.

Being out of my jurisdiction, there was not much more I could do. I thanked Special Agent Duval for all the information and leeway he had given me. "See you tomorrow morning at the FBI field office," I said as I went out the door.

"I'll see you at the press conference at 7:00 p.m.," he said.

"Right," I replied over my shoulder. "See you tonight then."

I went out to the parking lot, driving Erica's car to the Valley Hospital Medical Center. The hospital was just twenty minutes from the Vegan National office. The car's GPS provided the directions I needed. I took out my phone, preparing to call Erica, but then I decided to call the hospital directly instead, in case hospital protocol had required her to turn off her cell phone. I Googled the name of the hospital, opting to dial the number automatically. I then pressed the number option for the ER.

"ER. How may I help you?" asked a polite and professional female voice.

"Detective Erica Hunter was brought to the ER for a gunshot wound a few hours ago. Is she still with you?" I asked.

"No. The wound was superficial. She was just discharged and is now waiting for a ride home."

"That is exactly what I was checking to see."

"You'll find her in the lobby of the main entrance."

"Thank you for the information," I said, ending the call.

I was happy and relieved to know that Erica was all right. In retrospect, I realized she had played it safe when hit by the gunfire, deciding to play dead and remain completely still, rather than move and risk getting shot again. It was a tactic used in combat situations, and it had certainly paid off today.

Traffic was slow, and the pressure of the day began to slowly fade. My head started to hurt, and I realized that I was hungry. The pizza was great, but we'd eaten early, and with all the action throughout the afternoon, I was ready for dinner. I wondered if Erica would be up to going out for dinner, where she might want to go and if we would have time to eat before the press conference. I would have to wait and see what she had to say, and then we could make plans.

My mind then returned to the events of the afternoon, including my shock upon seeing the photo of Chef Patsy Williams and me on the wall. I needed to call Patsy to let her know the situation. I wanted her to be on her guard, but I did not want to frighten her unnecessarily, so I decided to notify her, but not talk to her in depth until I got back to Omaha. I needed to know more about the restaurant she and Chef Bob Dewey had co-owned in Vegas, along with Master Chef Pierre

LeJeune. There was something bothering me about this case; something was missing, or not quite right, and I needed to figure out what it was.

In the meantime, I called my boss and asked him to have patrols check on Patsy's home and restaurant every day, just as a precaution. This Vegan National group seemed pretty dangerous, and their leader, Daryl Parker, needed to be arrested for his criminal activities. I was not completely sure that this terrorist group had anything to do with the murder of Chef Bob Dewey, but it was our best lead so far. The two individuals arrested at the organization's Las Vegas office were in custody, and the FBI and DHS would grill them throughout the rest of the day and night. I hoped the raids on the other offices across the country would bring substantial information about our main suspect.

I called Erica from my cell phone, and she picked up right away.

"Are you going to be here soon, Seb?" she asked in a teasing tone.

"I'm stuck in traffic, but yes, I should be there soon. I am just five minutes away," I replied.

"Get here as soon as you can. I hate hospitals," she said. "They put me in a wheelchair, and they won't release me until someone picks me up."

"Okay. I'll put the siren on if the traffic doesn't break soon."

She laughed. "I'll be patient. How was everything at the crime scene?"

"Chaotic but fruitful. I will tell you all about it when I pick you up."

"Sounds good."

"Is the press conference on for 7:00 p.m.?"

"Yes. My boss set it up."

"Do you want to get something to eat first?"

"We won't have time, but I'm starving, and I'm sure you are too."

She knew me so well! I was famished. "Well, Detective Hunter, what should we do?"

"Let's go out. I don't want to be alone tonight, and I want to be brought up to speed on the case—on everything, not just what we tell the boss and the press."

"I'll take you wherever you wish. I'm ravenous. Do you feel like having meat?"

"I do, and I actually know the perfect place: El Calafate Parilla, in the Spanish Bay," she replied. "I'm sure you've heard of it; it's usually referred to as a Brazilian steak house, but the specialty there is Argentinean meats."

"Perfect! I love Argentinean food," I said, feeling my headache start to fade at the thought of the meal.

"I will call right now and make a reservation for 8:30 p.m.," Erica said. "That will give us plenty of time to do the press conference. Once you pick me up we'll need to go back to the station. My boss asked to see me."

"Okay. Make the reservation. I'm almost there; I see the hospital building. I'll pull up in front of the main entrance. See you in a few seconds."

We ended the call.

Ten minutes later we were on our way to the precinct.

Erica seemed fine and was in good spirits. She wanted to stop by her locker to change her shirt.

I told her I would go up to homicide and wait for her there. On my way up, I called Patsy at the restaurant. The dinner service in Omaha would be starting, and I wanted to catch her before she got too busy.

The phone rang a few times before connecting.

"La Cigale. This is Jenny. How may I help you?"

"Hi, Jenny. This is Chef Saint-Gemmes from the Drunken Frog. I need to talk to Patsy; please tell her it's urgent."

"Yes, Chef, please hold," Jenny replied.

"Thank you," I said.

Jenny was a very efficient hostess and had been with La Cigale for a few years. I had no doubt Patsy would promote her to management very soon. Perhaps Moose and I should steal her for our restaurant! I chuckled at the thought, which helped clear my head before I talked to Patsy.

"Seb, how are you doing?" Patsy asked when she picked up the phone.

"Doing okay, thank you. I should be home tomorrow evening, Patsy. We need to meet Wednesday morning at the precinct. You may be in danger. I am uncovering some pretty disturbing things here, and your name keeps coming up. How about 9:00 a.m.?"

"You're scaring me now Seb, but yes, I will meet you at the precinct on Wednesday at 9:00 a.m. What kind of things are you talking about?"

I tried to sum up what we had learned about Vegan National, the shoot-out, the foot chase, the people involved and the photo of Patsy and me taken in Omaha. I told her about the press conference, which she might be able to see later on CNN.

"I will ask Chief Lewis to assign a patrol car to your home and the restaurant, Patsy," I finished, keeping my tone reassuring.

"All right, Seb, whatever you think is best. Thank you. See you Wednesday morning."

"Have a great dinner service tonight, Patsy. See you soon," I said, ending the call and putting my phone away.

Erica approached me. "Come with me to the boss's office," she said.

I followed her there.

"Boss, this is Detective Saint-Gemmes from the Omaha PD. He's a certified executive chef, as you'll recall, and has been extremely valuable so far in the investigation of Chef Bob

Dewey's murder."

"Nice to finally meet you, Detective. I'm Captain Dan Hatchner."

"Nice to meet you, Captain," I said. "Thank you for having me here."

We shook hands.

"Thank you for your help," he said. "I'm glad to put a face to the name now." Turning to Erica, he said, "You okay, Hunter? How's the wing?"

"Fine. Thanks, Cap," Erica said quickly. "I'll be back on the job tomorrow. The doc cleared me."

"I got the paperwork. Take a day or two off if you need to."

Erica shook her head.

"Okay. If you're up to it, I'll see you in the morning. In the meantime, let's get this press conference over with." He put on his jacket, adding, "Time to feed fresh meat to the lions."

Chapter 20

The three of us went down to the first floor of the building at 6:59 p.m. A fairly large crowd of journalists was already waiting for us, and I noticed the logos of some national cable news stations, as well as the local affiliates of the major networks. I went to the right, away from the podium, as I did not plan on saying anything. This was Erica's show.

Captain Hatchner went up to the microphone, tapping it to make sure the volume was set. Erica stood at the captain's left side. She smiled at me, but I could see in her eyes that she was nervous. Who would not be, standing in front of the national press? Besides, there would only be a few minutes to discuss the case, and things were still up in the air. There would be a lot more information in the morning, following the ongoing investigations by the FBI and DHS, but Captain Hatchner had already scheduled the press conference, and the mayor wanted him to give information to the press.

Special Agent Gary Duval stepped up to the podium along with a man and woman I did not recognize, but assumed were local players.

"Good evening, ladies and gentlemen," said the captain. "For those of you who don't know me, I'm Captain Dan Hatchner of the LVMPD. You all know Christy Goldman, mayor of Las Vegas; Kyle Smith, chief of police; and Trevor Sulter, sheriff of Clark County. This is Special Agent Duval of the FBI. Here on my left is Erica Hunter, the detective in charge of the investigation into the murder of Chef Bob Dewey, owner of Tartufo at the Callegio Hotel and Casino. This press conference will take only ten minutes: five to give you the information we have as of now, and another five for questions and answers. Thank you." He turned toward the mayor. "Madam Mayor," he said, stepping back from the microphone.

Christy Goldman was a gorgeous woman, with blonde hair and a great sense of fashion. She had been at City Hall for the past three years and had done a decent job keeping the city sane. She appeared to be around fifty years old, and had the appearance of a Miss Nevada winner or a model. She adjusted the microphone as she looked at the crowd.

"Good evening, and thank you for coming at such short notice. I am not going to say much except that the entire hospitality industry of Las Vegas is mourning the loss of a great chef and businessperson. I can assure you that we will catch the individual responsible for Chef Bob Dewey's murder, and we will bring that person to justice. And now, I'll turn this over to the lead investigator, Detective Hunter from the LVMPD." She extended her arm toward Erica.

"Thank you, Madam Mayor," Erica said, after she stepped up to the microphone. "Good evening, everyone. I'm Erica Hunter; and, as you know from Mayor Goldman and Captain Hatchner, I'm the detective in charge of investigating the murder of Chef Bob Dewey. To summarize the situation, Chef Bob Dewey was found dead at his home on Saturday morning. He was discovered by the maid, who then called 911 at 10:30 a.m. A squad car responded to the call, followed by an EMT team. I was at the crime scene by 11:00 a.m. The medical examiner put the time of death at around 4:00 a.m. The entire house was searched by LVMPD, and CSI was dispatched to cover all the grounds. We know that the murderer came in from the rear of the house, through the park that abuts the property. He or she disabled the alarm system and then entered through the kitchen door. The cause of death is still under review, but I can tell you that Chef Dewey died by suffocation."

Erica was being cautious in not giving too much

information on the cause of death. Telling the world he had been force-fed corn mash—stuffed as a duck, in culinary terms—was not going to help the investigation at this point. Not too many women would have had the strength to pull off a crime of this nature, so by referring to the murderer as "he or she," Erica was deliberately not revealing to the press more information than was necessary.

"Chef Bob Dewey was an icon in the culinary world and a pioneer in the food industry here in the states," Erica continued. "His funeral will be held next Saturday, in New York. As for the suspects, the LVMPD in conjunction with the FBI, DHS, and the sheriff's department, conducted a raid a few hours ago, here in Las Vegas. Two individuals were taken into custody. They are persons of interest who seem to be involved in this case. We will be able to give you a lot more information tomorrow, following a morning meeting with the interested parties. A large amount of papers were found at the raid location, and the LVMPD and the FBI are going through them at this very moment. We believe the information gathered will help the investigation tremendously, but it is too early to get into specifics." She paused for a second, catching my eye. I surmised she wanted my support, so I nodded to her that she was doing a great job and should continue.

"That's all for now," Erica said. "I will take a few questions." She scanned the room, as all the reporters were raising their hands and yelling to ask their questions. She pointed to a lady in the front row.

"Thank you, Detective. Peggy Jones from KTNV-ABC News, Channel 13. You talked about a raid with the FBI and DHS. Why are federal agencies involved in a local murder?"

"Bob Dewey was a celebrity chef who had numerous restaurants in the United States," Erica said. "With the info found at the scene of the raid, we believe it may evolve to become a federal case, as it will cross state lines. As I said, I will have more information in the morning, after our meeting with the interested parties."

Erica pointed to a middle-aged man in the third row.

"Alexander Mendell, KWU-DIZ3 News. I heard from some of my sources that we may be talking about some local terrorism, even national terrorism—perhaps Daryl Parker, the leader of Vegan National. Is this true? Second, were you and two other LVMPD officers shot during the raid, Detective Hunter?" The man looked directly at Erica.

"To answer your second question, yes, I was shot in the arm, but as you can see, I am doing just fine. It happened when we surrounded the building where we apprehended the two persons of interest I mentioned. Two other officers were shot as well. Officer Delco is in fair condition, and Sergeant Mahoney is in critical condition. Both of them are at Mountain View Hospital. The shoot-out happened when the individuals attempted to flee the premises, despite our identifying ourselves. And for the record, the individuals we apprehended fired the first shots."

Erica took a breath and then continued. "As for your first question, we do not have enough evidence to comment on that for the moment. It is true that the raided office belongs to Vegan National, but we do not yet know if they are connected with Chef Bob Dewey's death. The investigation is ongoing, and we hope to have more information tomorrow. I believe—"

Mendell interrupted. "Detective, people need to know if there is a major threat to the city. We have the right to know!" His tone turned demanding. Clearly, he was attempting to agitate his fellow members of the media.

A few of them started to agree with him.

"Yeah, he's right! Let's have the truth. Freedom of the press guarantees our right to the truth!" said someone at the back of the room.

Another person said, "You are hiding something bigger.

The government is hiding a conspiracy! ..."

At that point, Erica spoke up, regaining control of the room.

"Please calm down," she said. "As I told you, this investigation is ongoing. We cannot give you more information at this time. And you, members of the media, cannot write or say anything that has not been confirmed. All you will accomplish is to frighten people unnecessarily. I know it is your job to keep the public informed, but please make sure that the information is accurate, not speculative. And, Mr. Mendell, I do not appreciate this rumbling of conspiracy theories. Please do not start any unfounded rumors. I told you all at the beginning of this press conference that more information will be available tomorrow. Thank you for your time."

Erica stepped away from the microphone and left the podium. I could see her angry expression as the captain stepped in to take over the microphone.

I followed Erica to the back door that led to an adjacent office. We went inside but left the door open.

"This case might be related to ones of bigger scope," the captain said, "But as Detective Hunter explained, we cannot say more about it now. We will let you know if any concrete news comes out. Mr. Mendell, may I have a private talk with you right now? Thank you, ladies and gentlemen. We will contact you tomorrow morning for another press conference."

Loud voices erupted, with more questions shouted at the captain.

"Captain Hatchner, is it true we are dealing with ecoterrorism?"

"Sir, are we talking about a chemical attack?"

"What should we say to our listeners?"

A uniformed officer was already at Mendell's side, motioning him to come to the back office.

"Don't touch me!" Mendell said in an arrogant tone,

even though the officer had not moved to lay a hand on him.

"This way, sir," said the officer, as he led the way to the back door where all of us had exited.

The members of the media were quite agitated, and most of them were tapping away on their phones and tablets, sending e-mails, texts and who knew what else. A frenzy was clearly starting.

The mayor, the sheriff, Agent Duval and Captain Hatchner all were now in the adjacent office.

As soon as Alexander Mendell entered the room Erica, now in the company of fellow members of law enforcement, was all over him.

"What is wrong with you, Mendell?" she asked, not masking the annoyance in her voice.

"What are you talking about, Detective? I am just doing my job! Of course, my source is confidential." His smirk matched his snarky tone perfectly.

"I will tell you what is confidential," Erica said, moving toward him so that her face was two inches from his. "Your information is not out there yet; so either you are just fishing, or you know something you shouldn't. There are only two ways you could know what you claim to know: first, there's a leak in the law enforcement community; second, you are involved or have contact with the terrorist."

"No! Wait a second here," Mendell sputtered, baffled by the sudden turn of events. "I am a member of the press, and you cannot accuse me of that."

"Why not?" Erica countered. "You love to spread rumors all around town all the time, with your so-called news, much of which has hurt some good people. Remember Superintendent Grassley and the supposed extramarital affair? An affair that did not ever even happen, but he lost his job, family and everything he had—all because of you. You are a mean motherfucker, and if you are in any way involved in this tragedy, I will take you down personally."

"You have no right to say any of this! You can't threaten me!" Mendell said.

At that moment Special Agent Duval turned toward the journalist. "You are a snake, Mendell," he said, raising his voice. "You are known in town for your paparazzi style and scandalous tales. I will keep an eye on you, and if I find out you are hiding anything or doing anything to impede a federal investigation, I will be happy to send you on a vacation paid for by the US government."

Captain Hatchner intervened at this point. "Mendell, stay in town, and don't report anything you might regret later."

"Is that another threat?" Mendell asked, his face bright red.

"Take it as you want," the captain replied. "But if a panic ensues, I'll know who started it, and I'll come after you." He nodded toward the uniformed officer, signaling him to escort Mendell out.

As the door closed behind the journalist, Agent Duval looked around the room. "We *are* dealing with some serious terrorists here," he said to all of us. "More than thirty people were arrested tonight in FBI raids across the country, most of them only small actors. Daryl Parker, our prime suspect, is still on the loose. All the intel seems to point to an attack somewhere in the country very soon."

Chapter 21

The Handler had decided to stay at the hotel for a few hours before heading out again. He planned to be on the road by two o'clock. After taking his time going over the information on the hit list that had been slipped under the door of his hotel room, he received a phone call from his boss, whom the Handler had come to think of as "the Mastermind."

"Our second target needs to be gone by Thursday, as planned," the Mastermind said over the phone. "Our third target will leave this earth on Saturday. That should give you sufficient time to organize yourself and obtain the equipment you need for each job. Once all three targets have been dealt with successfully, you will receive your two million dollars. Are we on the same page?"

"Absolutely," the Handler replied. "I am very familiar with the final destination. It should not be any problem."

"Good," said the Mastermind. "I will talk to you on Friday. Enjoy the road trip."

The line went dead, so the Handler put his cell phone back in his pocket.

He was actually getting excited about his move on the next target. He loved the city where he had to do this hit, and he already had plans for numerous visits to the many great restaurants in that locale.

The previous night he had gotten little rest, and the brief amount of sleep he'd had was uncomfortable at best. He wanted to reach his destination tonight, even if it was at a late hour; as he needed a power nap. Setting the alarm on his watch to wake him at 12:30 p.m., he lay down on the bed, closed his eyes, and drifted off to sleep, a smile on his face as he dreamed of the sumptuous vegetarian meals he would treat himself to while in the city of his next hit.

The alarm on his watch woke him at precisely 12:30 p.m., and he ordered some fruit, cottage cheese and sautéed vegetables from room service. While he waited for the food to arrive he went into the bathroom and took a shower. That always helped restore his energy. He turned on the TV, flipping the channel to CNN to check the news, but turning it off just as quickly when nothing seemed interesting to him. By the time the food arrived he was dressed and ready. He ate the food, packed his bag and left the hotel room at around 1:30 p.m., feeling rested and good. He went down in the elevator, checked out at the desk and then decided to get a coffee for the road. When checking in he'd noticed a trendy coffee bar in the hotel lobby, so he headed there now, ordered a medium-size black coffee to go and exited the hotel.

By 2:00 p.m. he was on the road, as planned, en route to his next destination. His rental Mercedes was such a comfortable car. He put on Sirius Satellite Radio, set it to Classic Rewind *so that he could listen to songs from the 1970s and '80s, and started to sing along as he cruised I-76. His mind started to wander, and he began to mentally plan his next assignment. He had a seven hour drive ahead of him, plenty of time to plan and organize, and then he could call his kids later, when it would be evening on the East Coast.*

He took a sip of his coffee and immediately spit it right back in the cup. The flavors were off, and the coffee had a burned taste to it.

"Why do people pay what they charge for this shit?" he muttered aloud. "Never again."

He wondered how the high-end coffee chain survived if this was the quality of its products, and yet their stores were all over the world. Fast-food dollar coffee tasted better than what he'd just sipped, and so did the coffee at most truck stops.

Now he was irritated, because he liked to have coffee on his road trips. He decided to take a coffee break in two to three hours, before getting on I-80 in Nebraska. Maybe he'd have better luck finding decent coffee in the Cornhusker State. He laughed out loud.

Looking at the skyscrapers of downtown Denver in his rearview mirror, his mind continued to wander. As the buildings receded from view, the Handler thought about his next victim and what he would do to it.

Chapter 22

Erica and I arrived at El Calafate Parilla, the restaurant in the Spanish Bay Resort and Casino, at 8:30 p.m. We were welcomed by a hosting couple dressed in tango costumes, as if getting ready to go out on the dance floor.

"Good evening. Do you have reservations?" the young lady asked. She spoke with a strong and exotic South American accent.

"Yes, two at 8:30 p.m., under Hunter," Erica replied with a smile.

"Please follow José to your table. Have a great meal."

We trailed behind the restaurant host, and I was blown away by the beauty of the decoration of the place. The walls were filled with framed black-and-white photos of Buenos Aires: the harbor, Puerto Madero, with its late nineteenth-century docks; La Boca, the iconic neighborhood, with its famous colorful houses; the legendary Argentine soccer team; San Telmo, one of the oldest neighborhoods in the city; the Palermo area, with its Italian influence, complete with trendy shops and restaurants. A beautiful wine cellar with more than two thousand bottles glowed by the bar area.

The aroma of grilled meat filled the air, and my stomach rumbled on cue. The early lunch pizza was long gone, I had plenty of room for food and this was the perfect place to refuel. The servers were all dressed in typical gaucho attire, and many of them looked as if they had just arrived from the pampas. There was tango music playing, with an accordion in the background. It brought me back to when Marie and I were first married. We'd visited my parents in Buenos Aires while my dad was working with the Argentine army in the 1990s. We loved the town, and we had the chance to visit many parts of the country. I felt like I was back in Europe because of the architecture in the city, but the immense open spaces made Buenos Aires very different from any European city. I found the city to be a great example of the mix between the Old World and modernity, with eighteen lanes of traffic across the Nueve de Julio Avenue and the beautiful Teatro Colón. The street made you feel like you were in Italy or Spain. It was such a great place to visit, especially for anyone wanting to enjoy the rich culture of immigrants, including fantastic food! (As for my parents, they were retired now, living in Santa Margherita in Liguria, Italy, where they enjoyed continuous warm weather, great gastronomy and beautiful sea views from their beach house. My little sister was an executive with a French company, and she lived with her family in Montreal, Canada. We were spread out all over the world, as a consequence of the family travel virus. My parents still had it, and they passed it on to my sister and me.)

José brought us to a large booth, and Erica and I sat down. Our server greeted us. Her name tag said she was Lucia from Chile.

"*¡Buenas noches!* My name is Lucia, and I will be your server tonight. Is this your first visit with us?" she asked with a great, professional smile.

"First time for the gentleman, but not for me. I have been here a few times already," Erica replied as she unfolded her napkin and placed it on her lap.

"Well, the concept is simple, sir," Lucia said as she turned toward me. "You have an appetizer and salad bar located behind this half wall; it is all you can eat. But, the best part is when the gauchos come to your table and offer you different kinds of meat or fish that were grilled on our barbecue, also called parilla or asado. On the table you will find a coaster with a green color on one side and a red color on the other. Green means, 'I want more'; red means, 'I am done for the moment.' Any questions, sir?"

"No, I got it. Pretty simple, like you said," I replied. "Can we see your wine list, please?"

"Here it is, sir," Lucia said, handing it to me. "Can I bring some water as well for both of you?"

"Yes, please," we both said.

After Lucia walked away, I told Erica that I had wanted to open a parilla like this in downtown Omaha. It was around the time Marie and I had separated, so I did not do it. I still felt disappointed by the missed opportunity. Omaha has always been a big steak-and-potatoes town, so I am sure it would have been a home run. To my surprise, we had many steak houses, but still no Brazilian or Argentinean parillas.

After going through the wine choices I opted for a wine called Structura Ultra, from the Bodegas Navarro Correas. It was a 2006, rated 90 points by Robert Parker. I explained to Erica the reason for my choice: the wine was a blend of Malbec, Cabernet Sauvignon and Merlot, all from the region of Mendoza, located in the beautiful foothills of the Andes Mountains, on the plains on the eastern side of Argentina. This wine region is the most important in production in South America, recognized as being at the forefront of new winemaking techniques and flavors. This blend was going to offer us a perfect blend of the Malbec, star grape of Argentina; Cabernet Sauvignon, with its tannin and oak flavors; and Merlot, with its medium-body attributes and berry-plum flavors. It was perfect for drinking now.

"Sounds good, Seb," Erica said, once again giving me one of her sexy looks.

We each smiled, clearly enjoying one another's company. The wine talk provided a nice diversion for both of us after the stress of the day, not to mention the shenanigans during the press conference.

Lucia brought the wine back to the table, and I asked her if we could have it decanted. It was a powerful wine that would certainly need time to breathe.

While our wine was attended to, Erica and I made our way to the appetizer buffet. The Italian and Spanish influences on the cuisine were very clear; the immigrants from those countries had clearly brought their food choices with them when arriving in Argentina. The buffet was filled with fresh salad, grilled asparagus, fresh tomatoes, mozzarella, olives, marinated anchovies, salami, cured meats, roasted bell peppers, cheeses, hearts of palm and many other traditional delicacies from Italy and Spain. The buffet could have been a meal in and of itself; and, the items were beautifully prepared. I wanted to leave room for the grilled meats though, so I went easy on the appetizers.

"We can always come back for more if we feel like it," Erica said.

We brought our appetizer plates back to our booth, each of us quiet while busily eating.

Everything was amazing so far. I could see and taste that it was all made fresh; nothing out of a can. It was a lot of work to prepare a buffet like this on a daily basis. I was impressed. It reminded me of the little trattorias in Italy, where they pushed the cart in front of you, offering six to seven choices. This was Las Vegas, so everything was gigantic, but in this case, quantity didn't trump quality. The food here was spot-on.

I lifted my glass to toast with Erica.

"To you," I said. "To being alive after this crazy day."

"Cheers to you as well, Seb," she said, touching her glass against mine. "And thank you for saving my life today." She winked at me.

We each swirled our wine, smelled it appreciatively and

then took a sip. It had the amazing flavors of ripe black grape, cedar and plum, with a hint of floral notes. It was definitely a full-bodied wine, with the perfect amount of tannins left, and a rich and velvety texture. The mouth feel was long, rich and intense. I could not wait to try it with my grilled meats.

After tasting the wine Erica said, "Yummy!" She reached into her pocket for her phone. "Let me check this text, in case it's work. Sorry, Seb."

"Don't apologize."

She read the text. "Gary just confirmed that the debriefing tomorrow will be at 8:00 a.m. in the FBI field office. Everybody will be on the call, from coast to coast. This is big." She put her phone away and finished her hearts of palm.

"Sounds good," I said. "I want to go back to Omaha with the maximum information possible. I already talked to Chef Patsy Williams. I told her to be careful. You never know with these psychos."

Erica nodded. "Based on what Gary said after the press conference, the manhunt for Daryl Parker is in full swing. It sounds like the feds searched the Denver area, and the last places he was spotted, but nothing so far. The two young fanatics we caught today are not answering any questions, but the night is just starting. They'll be ready to talk in the morning."

"I hope so. Information from them will help us understand how their organization works and what they have planned." I stopped talking as I saw a gaucho approaching our booth.

He offered meat on a big skewer, holding it aloft and parallel to our table. "This is vacio, marinated flank steak," he said, putting the sharp object on the green coaster, ready to serve.

"Yes, please, go ahead," I said, gesturing for him to serve Erica and me.

"It goes very well with the green Chimichurri in the tall bottle," he said, pointing to the glass container at the end of the table. "The acidity of the vinegar and the crunchiness of the shallots make this dish a delight."

The meat was, indeed, very well prepared in this case. It was medium rare to medium, and had a wonderful flavor. When working with red meat, the secret is to let it rest for a minimum of five minutes, allowing time for the meat to relax and reabsorb its own juices. If you cut red meat right after cooking it, blood will go everywhere. "Be patient," I always told my line cooks at the Drunken Frog. "It will be tastier if you do it this way; you need to respect the animal." I explained this to Erica as well. As with the wine, she seemed to appreciate the knowledge I shared, as well as the diversion from the case that the discussion provided.

"You're a real carnivore, Seb," she said with a laugh. "You really love your meat."

I grinned.

I then went on to tell her about how Moose and I had come up with our concept for the Drunken Frog. Our idea to create an American bistro and wine bar had come to us after we'd traveled to Chicago to attend the National Restaurant Association show. We went to an amazing eatery called Black Swine. The concept was based on the farm-to-table idea, meaning that the restaurant sought to use the maximum amount of locally grown and raised products. We were lucky to be based in Omaha, where there were plenty of farmers growing beautiful and tasty fruits and vegetables, producing flavorful cheeses and raising many different types of animals in free-range environments. Pork, lamb, beef and poultry all were easy to find, and they tasted amazing because of the non-GMO production. Moose and I bought the whole hog or lamb, and then we cut them in our own kitchen. From there we would decide what would be the special of the evening, served in small quantities or while supplies lasted, if necessary. Our food was always fresh, always prepared à la minute. Our menu offered many starters, often proposed in small sizes for multiple orders and sharing among guests. We also had a section in our menu called "Odds and Ends," which featured various cuts of meat, from the nose to the tail. We made our own blood sausage, using pigs' blood; we braised our own veal cheeks and smoked our own bacon. We also prepared all our charcuterie in-house. This gift from the gods was very popular in France, Italy and Spain, and we decided to produce them as a daily menu option, according to true European traditions. We did much research in order to re-create original recipes, such as saucisson, pancetta, chorizo, bresaola, duck prosciutto and coppa—and those were just a few of our selections. Our entrées offered every type of meat: veal, pork, lamb, beef, chicken, duck and fish, all prepared in many different ways. We seared, we stewed, we poached, we braised, we smoked, we fried, we boiled! All our great dishes were paired with an amazing full bar, craft beers and an eclectic wine list. Local craft beers like Lucky Bucket were customer favorites, and their product family paired very well with our gastro pub food. But, Nebraska was mainly known for its beef, and the meat I tasted so far tonight would give the Midwestern specialty some stiff competition. I said as much to Erica, a native Midwesterner, and she agreed.

The meat at El Calafate Parilla was so outstanding that I knew they had to import the beef directly from Argentina. The difference between American and Argentinean beef was the way the cattle were raised and fed. Most American cattle were confined in feed lots and fed a strict regimen of grain, like corn, to accelerate the growth of the animal in order to achieve maximum yield in a short time. It was pretty much the same diet fed to ducks prior to slaughter; ironic when you thought about it. In Argentina most of the cattle were raised free range, allowed to wander in the vast pampas, where they ate mostly grass. The taste at the end was very different, and I preferred the taste of Argentinean beef.

Tonight I was in heaven, even with a piece of meat that can be too chewy if not prepared correctly. After the vacio, came the mollejas, simple grilled sweetbread; morcillas, the equivalent of the French boudin noir (blood sausage); matambre, the meat located between the skin and rib of the cow; and Pamplona, chicken stuffed with ham, cheese and pepper. They also served us some goat meat, amazing leg of lamb and ribs. There were different kinds of fish also, as well as more-standard cuts of beef, but I preferred to eat the unusual asado dishes. I could have fish, ribeye, strip loin and tenderloin every day in Nebraska.

Erica agreed with this, digging into the asado samplings with gusto.

The evening ran its course, and I really enjoyed myself, savoring the opportunity to spend time with a great woman.

"How is your arm?" I asked her as I cut a piece of the lamb on my plate.

"It's fine," she said. "Does your shoulder still hurt from last night?"

"I hardly feel it," I said.

We smiled at each other.

"I'll take a last refill on the wine to finish my meat," she said, passing her glass to me.

I poured her some wine, and then I shared my thoughts on the irony about feeding American cattle the same diet as ducks in southwestern France.

"Interesting," she said. "I never knew that about corn."

We looked at each other. An image of Chef Bob Dewey suffocating on force-fed corn mash filled my mind. Erica's expression told me she was having similar thoughts.

"Let's not talk about the case any further tonight," I said.

"Good idea," she said. "Tell me more about the Drunken Frog."

"There is really nothing more to tell. I hope you will come to Omaha sometime, and I can give you the full tour, restaurant and all."

"I'd love that."

"So would I," I said. "I want to hear more about your plans, Erica. Do you want to stay in Vegas?"

"I'm not sure. I don't know if I really have a future here."

As our conversation got more personal, it felt like we were growing closer and closer. We had more in common than I'd ever realized. I so enjoyed just being with her, and I was glad it seemed she felt the same way about me.

After we had our coffee I paid the bill. We walked out of the restaurant and I decided to walk Erica to her car in the hotel parking lot. We walked hand in hand, and I gave her a good-night kiss on the cheek.

"See you in the morning," I said, but I did not step away from her.

Slowly but surely, she turned her head, gently pulling me back toward her and kissing me on the lips. Her lips were warm as we kissed for a few seconds.

She stepped back and got into her car.

"Good night, Sebastien. See you in the morning."

"Good night, Erica. Sleep well."

I closed her door, and she turned, giving me one last smile through the driver's side window as she pulled away.

There was definitely something happening between us.

Chapter 23

The 6:00 a.m. wake-up call was rough, but I got out of bed, took a quick shower to wake up my body, drank a large glass of water, ate a banana and decided to go for a run before the heat of the day made me change my mind. By 6:15 a.m. I was running along the trail in Cottonwood Canyon, at a pace of 8 miles per hour. My morning goal was 6 miles; I wanted to be back in my room by 7:00 a.m., so I'd have time to take another shower, get dressed and have breakfast downstairs. After some years of running, I realized that it made me feel better, not just physically, but mentally as well. It helped me keep my head straight. Of course it also kept me from feeling guilty about indulging in good food and wine. This morning's run would easily work off last night's big meal.

Throughout my run, I thought about the case and my return to Omaha. After I got back to my hotel room I jumped in the shower, and then I phoned Erica. We agreed to meet at the FBI office at 7:30 a.m. so we could get prime seats in the house. I quickly dressed and then headed downstairs to grab breakfast.

Erica and I arrived at the FBI office almost simultaneously. We walked through the parking lot together.

Special Agent Gary Duval greeted us at the entrance, ushering us inside.

Ramón Balusha, the head of the FBI field office, opened the debriefing. The introduction was quick and straight to the point. He thanked us for being there and then introduced all the parties in attendance: two members of DHS, the local director and his second; three agents from the Bureau of Alcohol, Tobacco, and Firearms (ATF); five officers of the LVMPD, including Erica, Captain Hatchner, and Chief Smith; three members of the sheriff's office; and one Secret Service agent. There were two men already seated at the far end of the room; they sat in silence and did not acknowledge any of us.

"Who are those guys?" I asked Agent Duval.

"CIA," he said

"CIA? Why?" I asked, taking another look at the dark suits.

"They always send their local boys when we talk about terrorism," he replied.

Erica and I then made the rounds, introducing ourselves to everybody. I handed my OPD card to everyone, as well as my restaurant card. I might need their assistance in the future, and food was always a good excuse for a meeting.

At exactly 8:00 a.m. the main screen on the wall of the room came to life. We could see four different split screens with the name of a different location under each one: Quantico, Virginia; Chicago, Illinois; New York, New York; Los Angeles, California. There was a video camera on the top filming us, so Las Vegas and the other four cities were all streaming live.

The room went silent, and someone at FBI headquarters in Quantico got up and started to speak. The camera zoomed in to focus on a man I did not recognize.

"Good morning, everyone. I'm Marshall Bain, Deputy Director of the Counterterrorism Unit for the FBI. I am based here in Quantico. The purpose of this meeting is to organize a task force with members from every law enforcement agency across the US. The goal of this task force is to arrest members of the group known as Vegan National. We also want to arrest the founder and leader, Daryl Parker. Stopping their activities is priority one."

A picture of a man in his forties appeared on the screen, along with some pertinent information: his date of birth, physical characteristics and last known address. "This is Daryl

Parker," said Deputy Director Bain. "Born in Portland, Oregon, in 1968; no siblings. His father was a farmer, but he left the picture early on. Parker was raised by a single mom. She worked in a meat-packing plant in Gresham, a suburb of Portland, to support herself and her son. Parker went to Oregon State University, but he never graduated. While there, he studied agricultural science and biochemistry, and had a high GPA. During his campus stay he was arrested a few times for animal-rights demonstrations. He created an organization called Pigs Anarchy, which was against swine production. From there his fanaticism evolved, and he used his skills in biochemistry to make homemade bombs to destroy facilities and equipment. Nothing could ever be pinned on him though, because he has a big underground following. His groupies always protect him. In 1995 he created Vegan National. Pro bono lawyers and other animal-rights groups, like ALF, helped him build it into a huge organization, with offices all across the country. As you know, Vegan National has a presence in many cities, currently launching attacks on companies and individuals involved in the food industry. The group believes in a strict vegan diet and is against any consumption of animal products and the facilities involved in such production. This is an extremely dangerous group of extremists whose tactics have recently escalated to violence and possibly murder. The irony of saving animals by killing humans has long been controversial. Ecoterrorism is now considered to be just another form of terrorism. We will hunt Daryl Parker down, find him and dismantle his organization. This group has been on our radar, but not as a priority. The recent events in Las Vegas have changed that, of course. Parker was last sighted near Denver, Colorado three months ago. We know he's in hiding now, but thanks to interagency cooperation, we are going to bring the collective resources and power of all our organizations to this case. As of this moment, consider Vegan National the most dangerous terrorist group in the country."

He paused for a second and then went on. "Local law enforcement will work with federal agencies—FBI, DHS, ATF—to take this group down. The FBI will interface with the Department of Agriculture, even though there's no representation from the department here today. Each FBI field office around the country will assign an agent in charge of the case, and each law enforcement organization will have a lead person responsible for reporting to the FBI office. The manhunt is already under way. We need to get these people. Thank you for your attention. You will all receive information about the coordinated effort by tomorrow, and that information will need to be dispatched to every member of your respective organizations. We will even ask for the help of the media in this matter."

Deputy Director Marshall Bain stepped back from the podium and slowly sat down. The camera zoomed out, and the FBI seal on the wall behind Bain filled the screen. I felt like a small fish in a big pond, and I made a mental note to contact Agent Carl Bruni, my friend and contact at the Omaha FBI field office, as soon as I got home. I was sure my boss would agree to let me be the OPD liaison to the FBI, since I was already involved in the case.

A few suits from all the different agencies spoke, assuring us that the interagency cooperation and coordination would be exemplary, as this group posed a great risk to national security. At 9:30 a.m. the video ended, and FBI Field Director Ramón Balusha asked us to stay put for a few more minutes to discuss the operations in Vegas. Erica was to be the LVMPD lead in this manhunt.

"Very good!" I thought to myself. Since there was a good chance that I would be the police contact for Omaha, Erica and I would have ample reason to continue to see each other.

Erica turned and smiled at me. It was obvious she was pleased with the decision, too.

Chapter 24

My plane was scheduled to leave McCarran International in Las Vegas at 2:35 p.m. That left time for me to have a quick lunch with Erica after she wrapped things up at LVMPD headquarters. I went back to the hotel to pack and check out, returning to the police station with my carry-on in the trunk of my rental car.

I called my boss in Omaha, told him what I had learned so far, and let him know that he would shortly receive more information from the FBI field office in Omaha. As anticipated, he agreed to let me be the person in charge of the case at the OPD level.

"Guess who the liaison is for OPD?" I asked Erica as she drove to our lunch destination.

"Who?" she asked with a teasing smile.

We both laughed.

I could tell she was as happy about it as I was.

We soon reached a little Mediterranean restaurant called Lebanon Kebab on Fremont Street. According to Erica, it was the best little gem in Vegas, with outstanding Middle Eastern cuisine.

"This is one of my favorite places," she said as she parked the car.

"That is good enough for me," I told her.

We got out and walked toward the front door of the restaurant.

I had a good friend in Omaha who lived in Lebanon for a long time. He'd shown me many photos of this beautiful country over the years, and he'd also cooked some traditional dishes for me to try: kibbeh nayyeh, the equivalent of French steak tartare and shish taouk, grilled chicken skewers marinated in olive oil, lemon, parsley and sumac. These dishes were amazing! I loved all the garlicky flavors, and the fresh-pressed lemon juice and extra-virgin olive oil complemented the spices perfectly.

We entered the restaurant, and the aroma of spices and grilled meats was tantalizing. I recognized the voice of Fairuz, the female vocalist, playing in the background. She was one of the most appreciated and beloved singers in Lebanon and the Arab world.

Aziz Ben Ali, the owner, welcomed us giving Erica a big hug and shaking my hand. I liked his sincere smile and felt comfortable immediately.

Erica introduced me as a cop who was also a chef and the co-owner of a restaurant.

"I have the *Best of Fairuz* in my car in Omaha," I told Aziz as he seated us at a table.

"I love her too," he said. "You have an accent. Where are you originally from?"

"Suburb of Paris, west side."

"I love Paris!" he replied with an even bigger smile. "I have a sister who lives in Meudon, in the south. I try to go back home every two years, and I always stop in the City of Lights. *Je parle bien le français,*" he added with a wink. "Make yourselves comfortable. I will prepare something special for you."

"Thank you, Aziz," Erica said.

I knew I did not have to worry about what was going to be served. The welcome from Aziz told me he would truly give us the best he had to offer. Besides, the flavors of the Middle East were among my favorites, always reminding me of my time in Paris, prior to moving to the states. There was a Turkish/Lebanese/Italian joint to the north of Paris, near Porte de la Chapelle. The Arabic music was always blasting, and the atmosphere, décor and smells made you feel like you could travel without needing a passport.

A few minutes later we had a mezze in front of us, with the usual mixed appetizers: baba ghanouj, a blend of roasted eggplant, tahini, lemon juice, olive oil and garlic; hummus, blended chickpeas, tahini, lemon juice, olive oil and garlic; tabbouleh, a salad of bulgur wheat, chopped parsley, tomatoes, mint, more olive oil and more lemon juice and falafel, the delicacy of warm-fired spiced ground chickpeas. A yogurt sauce, called lebneh, and some fresh pita bread were served on the side. Everything was fresh and super tasty; I was in heaven. It did not take a lot to get me there—just good food and wine.

After we finished our appetizers a variety of small items arrived, just enough for two people to sample: Daoub bacha, two lamb meatballs in tomato sauce; mfaraket, a spicy zucchini dish; maddous, stuffed eggplant in olive oil; and finally, the pièce de résistance, siyyadiyeh, a gorgeous red snapper cooked in saffron and served over a bed of flavorful rice made with sumac, served with a tahini sauce on the side. The entire dish was amazing; the fish was cooked spot-on, but the most wonderful thing about this dish was the perfect balance of spices, flavors and seasoning, all of which elevated it to another level. I thought that maybe Moose and I should open a Lebanese restaurant in Omaha. I needed to talk to him about that once I was back in town.

We finished everything on our plates and were definitely full. There was so much to eat that we'd barely had time for conversation.

Erica asked Aziz to bring us cardamom tea, and he insisted on giving us baklava for dessert. It was too much, but when it arrived, still warm from the oven, we could not resist.

"It is homemade and will be the best you have ever tasted," Aziz assured us.

He was right. The layers of filo dough, almonds, pistachios and honey, all dipped in a syrup made of rose water and sugar, had to be homemade. The pastry melted in my mouth, the perfect ending to a great lunch. I was glad I would be on an airplane soon; hopefully, I would catch up on some sleep. This sumptuous lunch would definitely help.

Erica and I knew we had to part soon, so we did not talk about the case.

"I'm going to come to Omaha soon, Seb," she said.

I was surprised and happy. "I thought we agreed we would not talk about the case."

"Not for the case, silly. For a visit. A *social* visit."

Now I was really happy. The adrenaline rush from the job was a big part of enjoying the past few days with her; I knew that. But I also realized my feelings for Erica went deeper than the rush of the job that I'd long grown used to, deeper than professional camaraderie and respect. There was a definite mutual attraction, and it seemed to be growing stronger. I sensed that she felt the same way. I hoped I was right about that.

At 12:30 p.m., I said good-bye to Erica, kissing her on both cheeks.

Just as she'd done the night before, she quickly moved her head to kiss me on the lips.

We kissed for several seconds, longer than we had last night.

"I will see you in Omaha, Seb," she said, with her eyes looking deep into mine. "Very soon," she added as she gave me another kiss.

My whole body shivered. There was no point in sidestepping any longer. I was starting to fall for Erica in a big way.

"You will be more than welcome," I said. "I will call you tomorrow to touch base on the case."

I saluted Aziz, thanking him for an amazing meal, and then I left the restaurant, got into my rental car and drove to the airport. My plane was leaving in two hours, and I had to drop off the rental car and get in line for TSA, a dreadful event for every flight.

But today, I didn't care. I was daydreaming about Erica and her visit to my home base.

Chapter 25

The Handler had arrived at his destination around eleven the night before. The trip went very well, and he had decided to stop every few hours to relax his legs and refresh his brain. Interstate 80 was definitely not the most scenic road, but he did not really care about that. He had listened to a mix of news and music, and then he'd called his kids on the East Coast, telling his daughter he was in route to Los Angeles. Celeste did not even question that he might not be telling her the truth. After ending the call, he'd felt bad about lying to her, but he quickly got past that. The less she knew, the safer she was.

When he woke up in the morning he ordered hotel room service for breakfast: black coffee, a bagel with cream cheese and a hard-boiled egg. He had checked into the hotel for two nights, hoping to reach Chicago on Thursday evening, after accomplishing his job here in the Cornhusker State.

By ten o'clock on Tuesday morning he was playing the tourist on Tenth Street and Howard, window-shopping and enjoying the architecture of the downtown area. He had actually visited this town with his family a few years back, during the College World Series. Arizona State had won the title that year at the Rosenblatt Stadium. Since then, a new arena had been built on the north end of downtown, bigger and better, and named after one of the biggest employers in town: TD Ameritrade Park. He'd enjoyed that trip immensely.

He decided to visit the Durham Museum to kill some time, learning quite a bit about the history of this Midwestern city, and the pain and suffering of the pioneers who had settled the area during the country's westward expansion in the mid-

nineteenth century.

By noon he was hungry, and he walked back to the heart of downtown. He arrived at his destination a few minutes later and stopped to check the menu posted in the window.

"Mussels Provençal with French fries," he murmured. "That sounds really good. Perfect with a nice local beer."

He opened the door, and a good-looking young woman greeted him.

"Hello, sir. How many people in your party today?"

"Just one, please," the Handler responded.

He sat down at a table in a beautifully decorated French restaurant in downtown Omaha, Nebraska: La Cigale, home of Certified Executive Chef Patsy Williams, the famous two-time winner of the James Beard Foundation Award for Outstanding Restaurant.

Chapter 26

My plane landed at Eppley Airfield, the airport serving Omaha and the vicinity, at 7:05 p.m., after two and a half hours in the air, plus the two-hour time difference with Sin City. By 7:45 p.m. I had parked my car downtown and was entering the Drunken Frog. I knew my shift was covered; I just wanted to check in with Moose and keep him updated on my situation and what was coming up. The restaurant was packed. Fleetwood Mac was headlining at the convention center tonight, and every time there was a big event in town all the downtown restaurants were busy. Tonight was no exception.

I quickly greeted the front staff as I made my way to the back of the house.

I tapped on the office door.

"Come!" Moose's voice came from the other side of the closed door.

I opened the door. "Hey, Moose. How is everything going?"

Moose sat in his chair paying bills. "Welcome back, my man," he said with a grin. "Busy … super busy, in fact. We have a full house, as I'm sure you saw. Thank you, Fleetwood Mac!"

I grinned, taking off my jacket.

"So, how was Vegas?"

"Pretty good," I replied, sitting down in my chair. "The food is always fantastic out there." He nodded in agreement, and then I added, "But the murder case of Chef Bob Dewey is getting bigger and bigger. It might be related to a national ecoterrorism case."

"That sounds like serious stuff, Seb," Moose said,

closing the folder with the bills and turning to give me his full attention. "You need more time off?"

"Well, I don't know yet. It will depend on what we find. All the law enforcement agencies are involved, local and federal, and we are being directed by the FBI. I am the contact person for OPD."

"Whatever you need, we'll work it out."

"Thanks, Moose," I said. "I owe you one, brother."

He shook his head. "Forget it."

"Patsy Williams's name came up a few times in the investigation, as did yours and mine, as a matter of fact," I told Moose. "There was also a photo of Patsy and me cooking at La Cigale, along with quite a bit of our personal information. We raided this ecoterrorism group's office in a Vegas suburb. It was really bizarre. This group is after people working in the food industry. I saw pictures of Anthony Bourdain, Daniel Boulud and plenty of other chefs. They were all contacted and warned about the situation. I need to talk to Patsy."

"She's lucky you're on the job, my man." Moose winked at me.

I laughed. "Yeah. For right now, put me on the line please; I need to think about something else."

"You are up!" he replied with a friendly smile. "I think Eduardo needs some help on the salad line tonight."

A few minutes later I had changed my clothes, washed my hands and put my chef coat on. I went behind the salad station.

The salad chef looked like he was in the weeds. He seemed relieved when he saw me appear at his side.

"¿Qué tal, Jefe Sebastián?"

"¿Qué es lo que necesita ahora?" I asked him.

"Mesa once, dieciocho, y veinticuatro."

For the next two hours we served a total of 150 customers. The evening started to wind down at around 9:30

p.m., and I decided I should talk to Patsy now, not wait for the morning. I did my reverence with the staff, told Moose I would call him in the morning, went to the back to change into my civilian clothes and headed to La Cigale. I walked slowly under the historical downtown cover, as I wanted to enjoy the gorgeous night.

Jenny recognized me as soon as I entered the French restaurant.

"Good evening, Chef. How are you tonight?"

"Good, Jenny, and you? Busy night tonight?" I asked her.

"Yes, we were, with the concert. Are you here to see Chef Williams?"

"Is she available, by any chance?"

"Yes. She should be in the back office. Go ahead; you know where it is."

"Thank you, Jenny," I said, walking toward the back of the house.

La Cigale was a beautiful eatery that had a lot of the characteristics of restaurants in the South of France. The walls were covered with a pale-yellow plaster that looked like the old cracked stucco of European buildings. Dried floral bouquets hung from the ceiling; the walls were filled with vintage posters depicting the Arles Roman Arena, the old harbor of Marseilles, Saint-Paul-de-Vence in Provence and other landmarks. The décor gave the restaurant a warm, nostalgic feel.

I passed the bathroom, located at the end of the restaurant, and then turned down a small corridor that ended in front of a door with a Private sign at the top. I stopped, knocked on the door three times, and waited.

"Come in!" I heard from the other side of the door.

"Good evening, Patsy. How are you doing tonight?" I asked as I walked in.

Patsy rose and approached the door, and we kissed on

both cheeks.

"I'm fine, Sebastien. How are you? How was your trip to Vegas?" She smiled warmly, but her face and eyes looked tired.

"As far as the restaurants go, it was perfect. The murder investigation was a little bumpier. Since you and I last spoke, the LVMPD discovered some weird stuff that might be connected with the crime. Do you have a second to talk now, or would you prefer to talk in the morning as planned? It is actually about the case."

"Yes, sure, now is fine, Seb. Give me one second to put these papers away, and I am all yours." She turned off her computer, put some bills in one of the drawers of her desk, and looked at me.

I took a deep breath, as I knew I was about to ask her some personal questions that might make her feel uncomfortable.

I sat down in the chair across from her, took out my notebook and pen, and put them on the desk.

"Patsy, this may be a lot to take in, so let me explain the best I can, and then you can ask questions if you don't understand," I said. She nodded, and I continued. "As I mentioned to you on the phone, the FBI got involved with the LVMPD's investigation, and we discovered an important network of ecoterrorists focused on people working in the food industry. I am talking about international food companies, restaurant chains, independent restaurants and chefs. Our names—yours, mine and Moose's—were on a map on one of the walls of the office of this group. There was also a photo of you and me cooking in the kitchen here in La Cigale."

Patsy's expression had appeared tired but pleased with the results of a busy day of hard work. After listening to me, her face shifted to a look of somber concern. "What are you saying exactly, Seb?" she asked slowly.

"I am saying that the danger to us may be greater than I

thought when I last spoke to you over the phone. There were dozens of names all over the map. Our names were the only ones in Omaha. In all of Nebraska, for that matter," I said. "The group is called Vegan National. Most of their offices are in the western states, with some presence in the Midwest. They have generally been active on the West Coast, and in states like Colorado, Montana and Idaho, disrupting production in factories by means of arson, vandalism and bomb threats. Up to now, no murders have been attributed to them—although there was a death as a result of arson—but at this point, everything points to them in regard to Bob Dewey's murder. They may have changed their policy, escalating to violence as a way to show they mean business. Groups like this often take extreme measures to promote their message. They can be extremely dangerous. A member of this group almost ran me over in a parking garage in Las Vegas, and he shot three cops the following day before I was able to apprehend him."

I stopped for a second, not wanting to overwhelm Patsy with all the details of the investigation. I could see she was shocked and frightened. She was not used to seeing and hearing this kind of stuff every day the way I was.

I continued in a softer voice. "Patsy, as I told you over the phone, I don't want to scare you, but you need to be careful until this case has been solved and the head of this eco-terrorist group is behind bars. Moose and I need to be equally careful. Don't open or close the restaurant alone, and don't walk to your car alone. Have one of the waiters walk with you. Can you do that for me, please?"

"I am not going to let any terrorists scare me!" she shouted, her loud voice surprising me. "I am still a strong woman who can defend herself. I will not change my life in response to this kind of threat. I have already been blackmailed and harassed by the Vegan Association and other animal-rights activists. I really don't like them, and I will fight them. I don't care!" She was now standing up behind her desk, her fists clenched.

"Patsy, please calm down. I understand your frustration. And you are right. It might be nothing. I just wanted to warn you of the potential danger, that's all."

"I appreciate that, Seb, really I do, and I'm sorry to have raised my voice. I will be more careful, for sure. I have a license to carry a handgun, and I will carry my gun from now on."

"All right," I said. "OPD is still going to patrol near your home and the restaurant, like I told you earlier."

She nodded. "Okay. Is there anything else you want to talk about? I need to get home. I have to be back early in the morning to prepare a seven-hour lamb roast, a great recipe inspired by my aunt!" she said with a big smile. "Stop by at lunch tomorrow, my treat."

"I think I will, Patsy. Thanks. But there is one more thing. I need to talk to you about your relationship with Chef Bob Dewey, especially when you worked together on *True Food Origin* for the Food Network, and afterward, when you co-owned Above the Stars, the restaurant at the King Arthur." I signaled her to sit back down.

"Yes, Bob and I were in both those ventures with Master Chef Pierre LeJeune. I thought I already told you about all of that, Seb. What more do you want to know? It was all a long time ago."

"I need to have the details, Patsy. It is important. Tell me about the show on the Food Network and the creation and closure of the restaurant."

"Well, Bob and I met during a food show in Chicago, twenty-odd years ago. We were sitting side by side during a seminar, and we hit it off right away. We became friends after that. I was working as the head chef for the Omni in downtown Miami at the time, and Bob was opening his second restaurant, Chanterelles, also in Miami. He was in town for five days, and he, Elizabeth and I all had dinner together one night. We talked for hours, and he told me the Food Network was interested in doing a show with him. He was not very certain about it, but after meeting me, he thought it would be great to do it together. He talked to his agent, who then contacted the network about my joining the team. Bob's agent negotiated for me too, and that's how *True Food Origin* was born. Master Chef LeJeune was signed to do the show shortly afterward. We started to tape a month later, all over the US. We visited all sorts of food-production facilities, focusing mostly on small producers and farmers. Big food companies refused to give us access with the camera. Personally, I would have loved doing some investigation on what was really going on in slaughterhouses and such places."

There was a glass of water on the desk, and Patsy reached for it, taking a few swallows. I could see she was starting to relax, thinking about the past, and remembering good times.

"It was the beginning of the Food Network at the time," she continued. "We had great success, and our show lasted for three years. Chef LeJeune was wonderful, but we never socialized. I became very good friends with Bob, though. We spent a lot of time together."

"Friendship, that's all it was?" I asked, keeping my tone professional.

"Yes. Elizabeth was very often with us, and they loved each other very much. I was dating the show's cameraman at the time."

"You never went back to television after that?" I asked.

"No. I wanted to open my own place. I had already been working for a long time, always in corporate hotels and big restaurants, and I wanted to do my own thing. So, a few months after the show ended, I got a call from Bob. He asked if I wanted to do something in Las Vegas. We met, and he told me that a new hotel/casino, the King Arthur, was scheduled to open, and they wanted to have a child-friendly restaurant owned by famous chefs. They planned to call the place Above the Stars. They already had Chef LeJeune lined up; they wanted a master chef, but he was pretty much a name-only person, rarely on the premises. It was understood that I would be the hands-on executive chef. I jumped at the chance, moving to Vegas so that I could be the main person on the job. Bob already had his restaurants in New York and Miami. But he was often in Vegas and was already thinking about opening an Italian place."

"He was an entrepreneur," I said, voicing my admiration for the man. "Already thinking about Tartufo even before the Callegio opened."

Patsy smiled. "Oh yes, Bob was always thinking about different projects. Always ready to jump into the next exciting opportunity, even before the latest one was off the ground." She paused and then added, "That is, until we had to close Above the Stars because of the lawsuit after the deaths of those two kids."

"Two kids died? Is that what you just said?" I asked, making sure I had heard her correctly.

Chapter 27

"Yes, two kids died of E. coli, and a few dozen people got sick from the contamination of meat that was not cooked thoroughly," Patsy said. There were tears in her eyes.

E. coli, a strain of bacteria harmless in the lower intestines of humans, was the bane of every chef when it contaminated food. The potentially deadly strains of the bacteria produced toxins that could attack the body in different areas: the guts, the kidneys and sometimes the nervous system. Some E. coli strains could cause clots to form in small blood vessels, leading to anemia. Extreme cases resulted in death. Not many outbreaks happened in the US, as the CDC in Atlanta was always quick to intervene and stop the distribution of contaminated products.

Patsy went on to explain how some raw contaminated beef from a Colorado plant was used in a meat loaf that was not cooked properly. At the time, the employee preparing the dish had messed up the timer, not realizing that the meat was not yet completely cooked in the middle. It was then served two days in a row to guests at the restaurant. Three days later, the health department came to inquire about complaints made by a dozen or so people. After an investigation, they realized that all the sick people had eaten the same dish. They took a sample of the meat loaf, threw away the rest, and shut down the restaurant. Above the Stars made the six o'clock news for a few days in a row, and the executives from the casino decided to close indefinitely as a result of the bad press.

I kept taking notes while Patsy talked.

"Many lawsuits followed, as you can imagine," Patsy

said. "And then, there was a deeper investigation after the death of the two children. Many weeks later, it was concluded that the contamination originated in the Colorado plant, as I mentioned; a carcass had fallen on the floor, but the meat had not been disinfected. The raw meat had then been ground as usual, and shipped from Colorado to Nevada, New Mexico, Arizona and California. Some instances of illness from the contaminated meat were reported in Los Angeles and Phoenix. The meat was then taken off the shelves of supermarkets and removed from restaurants. Luckily, nobody else died from the outbreak. Unfortunately, those two kids were casualties of negligence and training problems at every stage of meat production."

Patsy was now crying as she recollected the events. She wiped her eyes, drank some more water and continued. "Bob and I were not personally found guilty of anything, but the cook who ultimately recognized his mistake was fired by the casino management. The insurance company settled with everyone, which ended the lawsuits."

"It must have been terrible for you."

"Yes, it was. I still feel responsible for that tragedy." She wiped her nose with a tissue.

"I understand. People have no idea how important our job is, handling food on a daily basis. Training is key in this industry, and we need to improve the workforce, making them responsible for their actions." Patsy nodded in agreement, and I added, "But we both know that it is the owner who gets the short end of the stick. That is always the way in this business; it is one of the rules of the game."

"It's true," Patsy said.

"How did the parents of the children act with you and Chef Bob?"

"They knew it was an accident. The plant got a huge fine. The cook was fired and later convicted of manslaughter, with three years' probation. I met with the families, and Bob and I started an organization called Secure Our Food, Secure Our Kids. It was very successful—still is—and we've raised a lot of money that goes directly to fund culinary-safety education for aspiring cooks and chefs, as well as to help put pressure on the USDA to conduct more inspections at the different sites, to make sure all the products sold to wholesalers and consumers are disease-free. It is a huge task, as you can imagine, but it's worth the effort, even if we can just help a little bit."

"So, after the closure of the restaurant, you and Chef Bob drifted apart?" I asked.

"Yes, it was not a good time at all for me. But then one day I received a phone call from some developer in Omaha who invited me to open a restaurant in the downtown area, in this very spot that's now the home of La Cigale. You know the story from there, Seb. That was shortly before you and I met."

She looked at me, and I could see that she was feeling better, almost as if she'd had a weight on her chest all these years, and she was happy to at last be rid of it.

But I was not done.

"When did you resume contact with Chef Bob Dewey?" I asked.

"We were always in some indirect contact because of the organization we'd founded together, but we never did any promotional events together. He called to congratulate me the first time I won the James Beard Foundation Award for Outstanding Restaurant, and after that we started to see each other again."

"Was the conversation normal, or did you feel he might still have been affected by the restaurant fiasco?"

"He seemed fine; time had passed, and the wounds were healed. We were happy to do some work jointly again. So we started to do some events together here in Omaha, and also in New York and Miami, through our restaurants. That was when I introduced you to him here in town. I am sure you remember that day, Seb. You were as excited as a young man who'd just lost his virginity!" she said with a smile.

I laughed. "Yes, I do remember that. I became friends with Bob and Elizabeth. Are you going to the funeral in New York?" I asked her.

"Yes. I am scheduled to leave Friday morning, with a direct flight to La Guardia, and I will be back on Sunday night. Are you going?" she asked.

"I don't know yet. I have a lot of work here with the investigation, and I was scheduled to work the line this weekend. I'm sure Moose will be fine without me, but I'm the OPD liaison to the FBI on this case, so I need to play it by ear."

I looked down at my notes and saw I had one last question.

"Patsy, one more thing, and then I promise I will let you go," I said. "Did you ever get personal death threats?"

"Yes, I did, but only once. It really surprised me, because it came from a much-unexpected place."

Chapter 28

After spending an hour talking to Patsy I left La Cigale. We agreed to continue our conversation in the morning. I told her I would call her first thing to arrange a time.

I felt tired, as my day had begun early in Las Vegas and finished late in Omaha. When I finally arrived home it was 1:30 a.m. After taking a nice shower I got into my delicious bed. Unfortunately, at 2:00 a.m. I was still tossing and turning, and sleep would not come. The investigation was very much on my mind. Something about it kept bothering me, but I couldn't put my finger on what it was.

My mind drifted to my conversation with Patsy. I was still puzzled and bothered by something she had told me. She said she had received a letter from Germany written in perfect English. This letter, which had come to her through the attorney representing her in the Above the Stars lawsuit, accused the hotel/casino and restaurant of negligence. More specifically, the letter cited Patsy Williams, the executive chef in charge of the restaurant, as primarily responsible for the food contamination and tragic deaths. Death threats in the letter had prompted the attorney to contact the police. The LVMPD then contacted the FBI, which in turn contacted Interpol in Germany.

After a month of international investigation, the author of the letter, Friedrich Heinz, was apprehended in Munich and taken into police custody for authoring the death threats in the letter. And then, after only a few minutes of interrogation, Heinz told the whole story to the German police. Reports described that the man seemed very honest, relieved to have the opportunity to explain the whole situation.

The Heinz family was on vacation in the United States at the time of the incident. They'd arrived in Las Vegas from Los Angeles, where the dad, mom and three kids had just spent four days at Disneyland. They checked into the King Arthur Hotel and Casino, and then visited the Strip and downtown. During their stay they had dinner at Above the Stars, and everything seemed to be fine and without incident. It was not until a week after their return to Germany that Mrs. Heinz and one of the children, a boy, got extremely sick at the same time. Mr. Heinz called for an ambulance to take his wife and son to the hospital.

Mrs. Heinz was quickly diagnosed with kidney failure and blood poisoning. The poor lady suffered greatly, experiencing hallucinations and excruciating pain. She was hospitalized for more than six months, during which time she lost one of her kidneys and was paralyzed as a result of an infection that attacked the nerves and bones in the lower part of her body. The young son was luckier than his mother; he fought off the infection and fully recovered.

A year or so after their US vacation, Mr. Heinz received a letter of apology from the King Arthur Hotel and Casino regarding the E. coli outbreak; it was then that he realized the potential connection. Up to that point, he'd had no idea of what happened at the restaurant, as the news of the outbreak did not reach Europe. The Heinz family had traveled to the states independently, not with a tour, so there was no group Heinz could approach to lodge a formal complaint. He did his research, and asked the German doctors if the E. coli outbreak could have been related to the infection that his wife and son had suffered. The hospital told him that the E. coli strain identified in the Las Vegas outbreak had not been found in the system of his wife or son. In fact, the son had probably just caught a nasty bug, and that was why he recovered so quickly. The doctors insisted that it was pure coincidence that both of them had gotten sick at the same time.

Heinz was not happy, nor did he accept the answer. He contacted the hotel's law firm in an attempt to complain, accusing the restaurant and hotel of causing the bacterial contamination that infected his wife and son, causing his wife to become permanently ill and disabled. The law firm did not return his call. They sent him a letter advising him that he had no proof to substantiate his claims, so his accusation was baseless. The letter further stated that the mother and son had not eaten the contaminated food on the day the family dined in the restaurant. Heinz became furious. He was frustrated trying to deal with the problem from overseas and in a different language. He wanted to find a scapegoat and was determined to make it Above the Stars. That was when he finally sent the threatening letter that Patsy had described to me. It was addressed to the law firm, the King Arthur Hotel and Casino and Chef Patsy Williams. Heinz remembered Patsy because she had come out of the kitchen that night in her chef coat and hat, touring the dining room to greet the guests. She made a big fuss over all the kids, which had been a big hit with the Heinz children.

By 3:00 a.m. my mind was spinning like the wheels of my car. I turned on the light, took my notepad and pen from the drawer in the nightstand, and started to write my to-do list for the next day. I knew this would help calm my brain, and with any luck, I'd be able to get a few hours' sleep.

1) Call my cousin Michel, at Interpol in Paris, to inquire about the German connection;

2) Call Patsy to finish our interview, and remind her to bring the letter and all the paperwork from the lawsuit;

3) Call Moose for the schedule at the restaurant to see when I was supposed to work;

4) Book a flight to New York for Bob's funeral, and then clear time off with my boss;

5) Call Erica in Vegas for an update.

I looked at my list and decided to underline the first two items, which were the most important. I had to make those calls first thing in the morning in order to move forward with the investigation. I put the pen and notepad on the top of the nightstand and turned off the light. As I put my head on the pillow, I took two deep breaths and then finally fell asleep.

Chapter 29

My alarm went off at 5:45 a.m. with *Morning Edition* on NPR. I always enjoyed staying in bed for a few extra minutes listening to the news. Steve Inskeep and Renée Montagne now updated me on what had happened in our crazy world while I was sleeping. No major national or international catastrophes had occurred during the night, which was a good thing. I was not so sure what the news from Vegas would bring, nor the local news in Omaha, for that matter.

I slowly got out of bed and went to the kitchen to make some coffee. It was difficult for me to start the day without first having a short espresso, followed by a large mug of black coffee—fully roasted Black Mountain Colombian coffee, that is. The sudden smell of freshly roasted coffee beans rushed through my nose now, exciting my senses. I inhaled deeply, with the fondness and appreciation that only a true coffee lover can express. At that moment, my eyes brightened and my head started to clear. I made an espresso and set up the pot of coffee.

Thinking about my first call while I sipped, I continued to listen to the news as I scrolled through Contacts on my phone. "Michel Cell" showed on my screen. It was 1:15 p.m. in France right now. I lowered the volume of the radio and pressed Call.

After a few rings, it went to voice mail. The message, in French, said "Hello. You have reached Michel Caravaggio, Interpol Division Chief in Paris. I am not available right now. Please leave a message, and I will call you as soon as I can."

After the beep I said, also in French, "Hi, Michel, this is

your cousin Sebastien calling from Omaha. How are you doing? Hope the family is fine. This call is actually work related, having to do with a murder case I am working on here in the states. Please call me back at this number. Talk to you later."

It was only 6:15 a.m., so I decided to wait to call Patsy. She was an early bird, always the first one to arrive at the restaurant and never much later than 6:30 a.m. I knew she wouldn't listen to my advice about not opening alone, so I figured I would wait a bit and then call her. I wanted to finish the interview, get as much information from her as I could—including the letter and any other paperwork relative to the lawsuit—and then transmit all of it to Erica and Special Agent Duval in Las Vegas. The letter Patsy had described last night was particularly important. I felt we were getting close to a real break in the case, which was one I was eager to help close. I had made a promise to Elizabeth, and I intended to keep it.

I took another sip of coffee, sat down in front of the computer, and Googled prices on flights from Omaha to New York. After checking a few sites, I realized two things: first, it would be a long trip, with a least one stop; and second, it would not be cheap. Frustrated by the total inconvenience of flying out of Omaha, I wrote down the so-called better price and the site address, but I decided to go back during the day to book it. I was not in a hurry to spend five hundred dollars first thing in the morning.

It was now 6:35 a.m. I made another espresso, reached for my cell, scrolled through my Contacts and called La Cigale. I imagined Patsy was already at the restaurant, ignoring my warnings, just as I'd known she would. I understood why she loved to be there when it was absolutely quiet, no one talking, no phones ringing and most especially, no sounds from the ovens and the rest of the kitchen equipment. It was definitely a Zen moment for chefs; the calm before the storm, so to speak. It was similar to the amazing feeling when everything was ready on the line for the dinner service, and we stood waiting for the first ticket to spit out of the printer. Almost like soldiers trained and ready to fight, in position on the battlefield awaiting the first shot. When the first ticket arrived, all hell would break loose, and the adrenaline rush would start—the only difference was that cooks on the line didn't get shot at. Maybe I only thought of the two as similar because I was a chef *and* a cop.

I chuckled to myself, sipping more espresso as I listened to the restaurant's message: "Thank you for calling La Cigale, located in downtown Omaha. We are open Monday through Saturday, from 11:00 a.m. to 11:00 p.m. If you would like to make a reservation, please leave a message; or, you can book a table online, at LaCigaleOmaha.com. Thank you and have a great day."

After the beep, I said into the phone, "Good morning, Patsy, this is Sebastien. Are you there? Please pick up the phone if you can hear me." I waited a few seconds to see if she was going to pick up, but she didn't. "Patsy, I will try to call you later, or you can call me if you want. I would like to finish our interview before we both get busy for the day. Talk to you soon."

I ended the call, knowing that her first employee would arrive by 8:00 a.m. to start the lunch prep. If I didn't hear from her in fifteen minutes or so, I would call again.

I sent a quick text to Moose, asking him what the weekend schedule was, so I could make my plans to fly to New York for the funeral. I knew there wouldn't be any problem, but I wanted to play fair and not put Moose or the staff in a bind. Moose had always been so kind and understanding regarding my schedule at the restaurant. There were enough people working the line at every shift, so he didn't really need me. But, he knew working the line was my second passion, and I needed the release to ease the tension of my full-time detective job. He made it work because he wanted to help me. Man, what a great friend! I would do the same for him, and he knew it.

After finishing my second espresso, I started on my mug of Black Mountain Colombian, noting that I had crossed four out of five things off my list, without really achieving any of them. I decided to wait to call Erica until later in the morning because of the time difference, hoping that I would be able to deliver more information to her by that point, perhaps even some new leads in the case, once I got the letter from Patsy.

I went upstairs, put on my running clothes, jogged downstairs, ate a protein bar and drank a glass of water.

I tried Patsy again, at the restaurant and on her cell; still no answer. I figured she had probably decided that she would call me later. I left a message on her cell's voice mail: "Patsy, this is Sebastien. Please call me when you get this."

Five minutes later I was headed for the running trail near my house. It was 6:50 a.m.

Chapter 30

The Handler's day began at 5:00 a.m. with a wake-up call from the front desk. He got out of bed pretty quickly, as he always had trouble sleeping before a job. His thoughts immediately went to Celeste. He loved his daughter dearly, and he'd missed her greatly during the past year. He would be home soon; he could hardly wait. Jumping into the shower while his coffee brewed in his room, he started running through the plan in his head. He needed to be smart and work fast. The window of opportunity was short, and he could not fail. He had done enough morning surveillance to know his target had a consistent routine. Nevertheless, he had rehearsed a plan B, just in case something came up unexpectedly.

He put on the TV as he drank his coffee and got dressed. The weather was supposed to be great all day, and he was glad with the long drive ahead of him. He packed his bag and then made sure to wipe as many of his prints as possible, as well as removing whatever other traces could be linked to him from his stay at that hotel.

He went down to the lobby and walked up to the front desk.

"Good morning, Mr. Smith. How was your night with us?" the clerk asked, flashing a bright smile. "Checking out this morning?"

"Yes, please. I have a long drive ahead of me this morning, and I want an early start. I hope to be on the road before anyone else."

"My father always said, 'The day is owned by the person who starts very early,'" the clerk responded, handing the invoice

to the Handler. "Where are you headed, sir?"

"St. Louis first, and then Louisville, Kentucky, by the weekend." He handed a credit card to the clerk.

"Thank you, Mr. Smith. Here is your card. We appreciate your choosing us for your stay, and have a safe trip."

The Handler took his card back, said good-bye and walked toward the complimentary coffee stand just inside the hotel entrance. He filled a to-go cup, picked up a muffin and a banana and was ready to hit the road.

It was 5:45 a.m., so he had a few minutes to get things ready. He went to his rental car, opened the trunk and put his overnight bag inside. He pulled out another bag so that he could check the instruments he would need for the job. Closing the trunk, he took the bag and his breakfast with him to the front of the car, opened the driver's side door and got inside. He put the bag on the front passenger seat. After carefully checking the contents of the bag he felt satisfied and confident; everything was in place. He pulled out the map of downtown Omaha that he had printed the night before in the business office of the hotel, looking at the getaway road for the hundredth time. He knew exactly where to park his car: the perfect position to enable him to be on the highway within thirty seconds of finishing the job. He would then be across the state line in Iowa less than three minutes after starting the engine of the Mercedes. He had calculated the walking time it would take to go to and from the site of the job, and he knew that the downtown area was pretty deserted in the early morning hours. He had already checked that out during his morning surveillance.

The Handler was a very precise man who calculated every angle and prepared for every eventuality. He was ready.

He stayed in his car for another ten minutes, savoring his coffee and muffin. He decided to save the banana for later. At 6:05 a.m. he started the engine. He smiled as he passed the beautiful First National Bank of Omaha building, still illuminated by its nighttime lights. Enjoying the emptiness of the streets at this early hour—with the exception of the city cleaning crew which paid him no mind—he easily parked on Thirteenth Street. The parking meter would not start until 8:00 a.m., and he would be long gone by then.

A creature of habit, he checked all his gear one more time, got out of the car and started to walk along the still-dark alley, crossing to Twelfth and then Eleventh Street. The alley was almost pitch-black, but he had studied the details for many hours throughout the past year, in addition to doing his surveillance work over the past few days, so he could have walked to his destination blindfolded. The entire area seemed deserted; not even a downtown security guard was in sight.

The Handler smiled. He arrived at the back door of his destination, where he hid behind a very large commercial trash container.

He glanced at his watch: 6:15 a.m. He had about fifteen minutes to wait.

He looked at the door on the other side of the trash container, reading the sign: La Cigale—Deliveries and Employee Entrance.

Target number two was about to be eliminated.

Chapter 31

My morning run was a real pleasure, as the early hour kept the air fresh and cool. My goal was a simple six miles that I planned to run in forty-five minutes. My headphones were on, and I was listening to my favorite group, U2, and remembering the first time I saw them in concert, in Kansas City, almost two decades ago. Two friends and I made a road trip from Omaha, driving there in one night. We had a blast in the packed arena, and the band played all my favorite tunes. My mother and aunt had given me my first U2 album when I was twelve years old, and I was hooked. I've followed the stories of all four members of the group ever since. I liked the fact that the band was still intact, entertaining "old folks" like me, as my son was fond of telling me.

As I was enjoying "Where the Streets Have No Name," I felt my phone vibrate on my arm. Without stopping my run, I checked the screen and saw the phone number of OPD headquarters. I made a face; I'd hoped it would be Patsy, returning either one of my calls. I pressed the On button, and the music stopped playing, giving way to a short silence before my boss's voice came alive.

"Saint-Gemmes?" Randy Lewis said in a sharp voice.

"Yes, Boss. What can I do for you?" I replied, trying to keep my pace and heart rate at regular levels to avoid running out of steam.

"We just got a call from La Cigale restaurant. It's not good, Sebastien."

I stopped my run in two steps, coming to an abrupt halt. My heart was racing like I'd just finished a 200-meter race.

Silence was all around me, as my headphones muffled the sounds of the wooded park and the morning traffic. I could hear Randy's breathing on the other end of the line.

"You're still with me, Saint-Gemmes?"

"Yes, Boss, I am here."

"A cook from La Cigale called at 7:50 a.m., after he arrived on the scene. The restaurant was open but appeared to be empty. At first, he thought he'd find his boss in her office, but she wasn't there. Then he thought maybe she was in the bathroom, but she didn't respond when he knocked on the door or called out to her. She was nowhere to be found, so he quickly realized that something was wrong. As he entered the walk-in fridge, he found a body in pool of blood; everything was covered with a white substance, also marked with blood. Panicked, he called 911 and told the operator what he had discovered."

"Was it Patsy?" I asked hurriedly, my fear of a disaster rising.

"Well, he thinks so. The first patrol just arrived, and we don't yet know exactly what is going on. The officers called for backup and the fire department. I told them to wait for you and the EMTs before touching anything. Brian O'Toole was the first officer on the scene. When can you get there?" Randy's voice held a tone of urgency.

I looked at my watch: exactly 8:00 a.m.

"I'll be there in fifteen minutes. Please make sure they follow your instructions and do not touch or disturb anything. Thank you, Boss."

I ended the call and sprinted back to my house. I think I beat my personal six-mile record on the last mile. At 8:05 a.m. I was in my car, with my siren blasting, racing through the packed streets of the morning rush hour. Commuters heading downtown moved to clear a path for me.

How I wished I had not waited for Patsy to call me back

after I left the messages. If only I'd just headed to the restaurant! I knew that such thinking would accomplish nothing—except perhaps to dilute my focus and make me ineffective at the time when I most needed to be at my best on the job. So, I put all my energy into the investigation.

While driving I called Brian O'Toole. He was a veteran with fifteen years on the force, and we had worked together on several cases over the years. He was very good at his job, and I knew he would quarantine the scene until my arrival, following the instructions of the OPD chief himself.

"Sergeant O'Toole speaking," said my colleague when he answered his phone.

"Sergeant, this is Detective Sebastien Saint-Gemmes. I will be the lead person at this crime scene," I told him.

"Yes, Detective. The chief called and told us. What can I do for you now?" he asked.

"You are my eyes on the ground right now. Are the fire department and EMTs already there?

"No, not yet; they should be here any minute."

"I know the layout of that kitchen very well, but can you tell me what you see? Does anything look out of place?" I could visualize the cooking line of La Cigale, with its two 10-burners, four convection ovens, three-footer flat grill and double fryer. On the opposite side was the plating area, a large and long refrigerated prep table, with a heat lamp to keep the food hot until the server took the plates to the tables in the dining room.

"Nothing really looks out of place in the main kitchen, Detective."

"Okay," I said. "Let's move toward the dish room, please."

"Well, nothing out of the ordinary here either," said the sergeant. "The place is spotless." He sounded impressed.

"That's Patsy for you," I said. "A clean freak with an impeccable kitchen where you could eat off the floor."

I remembered well Patsy telling me that she wanted the back of her house to always be immaculate. She had worked in some shady places at the start of her career, and she promised herself that if she ever had a restaurant of her own, she would put Mr. Clean himself to shame.

"I'm coming up to the pantry, Detective," Brian said now. "It looks like there was some movement here ... some shelves are empty, but I cannot figure out what's missing."

"All right. Now go to the walk-in fridge, but don't enter it. Just open the door. Tell me what you see."

"Okay."

"Be careful and gentle," I added. "Put some gloves on; I'm sure you can find some on the cooking line."

I could hear the snap of latex against skin, and I pictured Sergeant O'Toole slowly approaching the fridge.

"All right, Detective," said the sergeant. "I'm opening the door now."

I could hear the sergeant's breathing, and in the background, the noise of the cooling system of the chamber. The seal of the door as he opened it created a louder sound, and then I heard him gasp.

"Oh my God! Oh my God!" the sergeant said over the phone. The next sound was that of a six-foot-three veteran police officer throwing up.

Chapter 32

At 8:18 a.m. I pulled up in front of La Cigale, where flashing lights from police cars, EMT vehicles and fire trucks created a surreal atmosphere in the area. Actually, *surreal* was an underestimation of the scene. All of Thirteenth Street was blocked with emergency vehicles, and the flashing lights painted a chaotic moving pattern along the walls of the buildings. I cut the engine, got out of my car and started to walk toward the old brick building. The Drunken Frog was not even a block away, and I was accustomed to seeing this street full of diners and tourists, not fire engines and cop cars.

From a distance, I saw my boss talking to the fire chief. Randy seemed pretty agitated. When he saw me, he excused himself and started to walk toward me.

"Good morning, Detective," he said. "The situation is under control. The building is clear. CSI just arrived, and they are getting ready to go in. Sergeant O'Toole is waiting for you outside the restaurant."

All of a sudden, I felt nauseated. It was my fear coming through; I was afraid because I expected the worst. As I walked toward La Cigale, I took some deep breaths. I felt calmer, and the nausea subsided. Before approaching the restaurant's entrance, I put plastic coverings on my shoes in order to avoid contaminating the crime scene.

Sergeant O'Toole was sitting on the floor right in front of the entrance to the restaurant. He got up as soon as he saw me.

I greeted him, noting how pale he looked.

"Detective, it is not pretty. Whoever did this had a real

grudge against the victim."

"You don't look too good, Sergeant," I said. "Go drink some water and then take a walk."

As Sergeant O'Toole walked away, I headed toward the CSI team.

The medical examiner, Roger Pearson, stood beside CSI Duane Pollock and CSI Jerome Jund. They each carried bags containing the tools of their respective trades.

All four of us stood in front of the revolving door that served as the main entrance to the restaurant.

"Good morning Detective," said CSI Jund, better known to his colleagues as J. J.

"Good morning guys," I said, including all of them.

"Morning," Roger and Duane said in unison.

"Sergeant O'Toole says it's bad, one of the worst he's ever seen," J. J. said.

"They're all bad," said Roger.

I agreed with the ME. "Let's just get to it."

I led the way to the walk-in fridge, walking slowly to avoid disturbing any potential clues, and the ME and CSI team followed close behind me. I stepped aside, letting them go in first.

I mentally prepared myself for the shock of what I was about to see. But I soon realized nothing could have prepared me—or anyone—for what we found.

"Oh my God!" I said, echoing the reaction of Sergeant O'Toole while he was on the phone with me. Now I understood why he couldn't manage to say anything else, why this crime scene had so viscerally impacted a veteran police officer.

The body was in a fetal position, covered in a white substance mixed with blood. The blood was now dark purple. The only thing not covered in white was the face of Chef Patsy Williams. Her eyes were wide open, fixed in my direction. I could clearly see that her throat had been slashed from one ear to the other. Her head lay in a large pool of blood, and she looked tiny, possibly because she was curled up. A heavy cast-iron pot sat on the floor beside the red puddle, seeming out of place.

Duane took photos of the body from various angles, as well as some shots of the entire inside of the fridge.

J. J. took a sample of the white substance and placed it in an evidence bag.

Kneeling down, I looked at the substance, trying to figure out what it was. I touched some of it, feeling the crystalline texture, and put a fingertip-size amount on my tongue. As I'd suspected from touching it, it was kosher salt, which Moose and I used in our restaurant too.

"I'm so sorry, Sebastien," J. J. said.

"As am I," said Roger. "I know you were close to Patsy Williams. I will do my best to get as much information to you as soon as possible. I'll call you as soon as I know the cause of death."

"Don't worry," said Duane. "We will get this guy,"

Two EMTs came into the kitchen pushing a stretcher. They waited for orders from the ME. Meanwhile, the forensics team took photos and dusted for fingerprints on the inside and outside of the walk-in fridge, as well as various surfaces throughout the kitchen—anywhere that the killer might have left a print.

After the ME and CSI had spent half an hour with the body, CSI started to remove the large amount of salt poured over it. The blood had already started to dry, forming hard, dark-purple chunks. As J. J. began putting the salt in larger evidence bags than he'd used for the sample, the ME and I realized that the body was not actually in the fetal position.

We looked at each other in horror once the salt was removed and we could see that all the joints in the body had been broken, extracted and piled on top of the torso.

"What in the world?!" I shouted.

The rest of the CSI team turned their heads in my direction.

"This guy is sick," I said. "I really hope he did not do that while she was still alive."

"I think it was done postmortem, because of the marks on the body," the ME said. "I will have to confirm that once I get her into autopsy, but it looks that way to me. What troubles me is, why put salt on her like that?"

I had an idea, but I wanted to keep it to myself a little longer.

I was freezing cold from being in the fridge all that time, but that didn't cool my anger one bit. I was furious. What kind of monster could commit such a horrible crime?

First, Chef Bob Dewey in Las Vegas; now, Chef Patsy Williams in Omaha. Two chefs brutally murdered in less than a week was no coincidence—especially since they had a personal connection.

I needed a second to think and breathe, which was difficult to do in the extreme cold. "Call me as soon as you have something, please," I said to Roger and J. J., and then I walked out of the fridge.

I went through the kitchen and out to the dining room, where a few cooks waited. I surmised that they had arrived for the morning production and Sergeant O'Toole had told them to gather in the dining room until an officer took their statements. I recognized Enrique from El Salvador, who was in charge of the pasta; I also knew Pedro from Mexico, who was in charge of the stews on the menu. I did not know the others. They all looked at me with confused stares.

"*Hola, Jefe Sebastián,*" said Pedro. "*¿Qué pasó aquí?*"

"Good morning, guys. Did you hear anything from Chef Patsy Williams before you got here?" I asked them in Spanish.

"No," said Pedro, relating in Spanish what had

happened. "We just showed up for our regular shift. The cops let us come in because we are part of the staff and they wanted to ask us questions. They asked us to stay here for another ten minutes to give our statements. I left at five o'clock yesterday, before the dinner service. I think Enrique left before me." Enrique nodded that this was correct.

They were part of the prep team, and they also worked the lunch service, so this made sense.

Continuing to speak to them in Spanish, I said, "Thanks, guys. I will keep you updated on what's going on later; stick around for questioning, but I am sure you will be off for the rest of the week … if not longer."

As I exited the restaurant I pulled out my phone, scrolled through Contacts, and called Erica's number. It was very early in the morning in Vegas, but I needed to tell her about the most recent victim, especially the gruesome method of the murder, which was even worse than what had been done to Chef Bob Dewey. We needed to stop this maniac's killing spree—and fast.

I did not yet know who the killer was, but I was pretty sure I knew who the third victim would be.

Chapter 33

The phone rang three times, and then voice mail answered. I left a message for Erica, asking her to call me back as soon as possible.

"Chef Patsy Williams was murdered in Omaha early this morning," I said before ending the call.

I put my phone back in my pocket and walked toward my boss to share my suspicions regarding the likely third victim.

"You sure, Detective?" asked Randy Lewis, his tone serious.

"I'm pretty sure, Boss, but I need to double-check a few things with Detective Erica Hunter in Las Vegas. She is the detective in charge of the Chef Bob Dewey case, and my counterpart police liaison to the FBI on the ecoterrorism situation as well. I left a message for Detective Hunter, and I'm about to call my local FBI contact here in Omaha. I'm sure the feds will be interested in hearing about the murder of Chef Williams."

Randy nodded. "Do what you have to do. Just keep me posted."

I signaled that I would, turned, and pulled out my phone once again, this time to call Agent Carl Bruni in the Omaha FBI field office.

He picked up after the first ring. "FBI Omaha, Agent Bruni speaking."

"Good morning, Agent Bruni, this is Detective Sebastien Saint-Gemmes from OPD. We have a situation here downtown that I am sure you will be interested to hear about. Chef Patsy Williams has been killed, and it looks like a similar pattern to our murder in Las Vegas."

"What happened, Detective?" he asked.

I related all the gory details of the crime scene, including the similarity between the murders in the two cities. I finished by sharing my suspicions as to the likely third victim.

Agent Bruni indicated he'd been briefed by his superiors regarding the ecoterrorism situation; he knew I was the OPD liaison. "I will be there in ten minutes," he said. "I am already out of the building."

The FBI field office was located at the intersection of two highways in the heart of Omaha. If Agent Bruni had his sirens on all the way, I knew it would take him less than that amount of time.

I then called Ben Oswald, a friend at the traffic unit of the OPD, hoping we could get some surveillance video of the area around La Cigale from early this morning. Ben was actually the head of the department; he was very cool and a lot of fun.

He picked up the phone right away. "Ben Oswald speaking."

"Good morning, Ben, this is Sebastien Saint-Gemmes. How are you doing this morning? How are Marsha and the kids?"

"Great! How are you doing? Still single?" He chuckled. "What can I do for you, Sebastien?"

"Well, we had a 187 at La Cigale restaurant on Thirteenth Street early this morning. I need footage from the camera positioned between Tenth and Fifteenth Streets, and also from Dodge and Leavenworth. Whatever video you have from between 12:00 a.m. and 8:00 a.m. today, please. It is an emergency; I am hoping our murderer was caught on camera."

"I'm on it. I will call you when it's ready; give me thirty minutes," he said before hanging up.

Next, I needed to talk to the Iowa State Patrol, as I was pretty sure our manhunt was going to cross the Cornhusker

State. I went back to Randy to ask him the name of the person in the Council Bluffs office who could answer my questions and raise the alarm in case my theory was correct.

"Talk to Major Tyron Bell," Randy said. "He's second in command for the Iowa State Patrol in the Council Bluffs area. He should be able to help you, or at least listen to your concerns."

I called dispatch from my car and requested to be put through. The switchboard answered after one ring.

"Iowa State Patrol, Council Bluffs. How may I direct your call?"

"Major Tyron Bell, please. This is Detective Saint-Gemmes from the Omaha Police Department, and it's an emergency. Thank you."

"Hold on please."

A few seconds passed, which gave me a chance to look at my watch: it was not even nine o'clock in the morning.

"Major Bell speaking. What can I do for you, Detective?" he asked when he got on the line.

"Good morning, Major. Thank you for taking my call. We have a situation here in Omaha, which is likely tied to another crime in Las Vegas. Both are brutal murders. The FBI is on the Las Vegas case as well, suspecting a national terrorist group is behind the killing. Local FBI is on the way to the crime scene here, even as we speak. I'm calling you because I believe our killer is on I-80, headed east. I'm waiting on information regarding a description of the vehicle, and hopefully, a license plate. I just wanted to warn you about a potential terrorist crossing into your state. If you contact your local FBI I am sure you will receive further details. My understanding is that all field offices are on alert."

"Yes, I've already received a communiqué, but I didn't expect a murderer/terrorist to be crossing into my state so soon. Thank you for the heads-up. I will put all troopers on alert, letting them know they should be prepared to act appropriately. I will wait for your call regarding the vehicle description and plates."

"You will have that info as soon as I receive it, Major."

We ended the call, and just as I was putting my phone away I saw a black SUV that looked like FBI, followed by a second identical vehicle. Both vehicles stopped near the fire trucks, and a total of five men got out. This was official FBI business.

Agent Carl Bruni waved to me. He and his crew were dressed in khakis and blue polo shirts, over which they wore FBI vests; their guns were holstered. I had known Carl for many years. Although he was a native of Lincoln, Nebraska's capital, he hoped to be promoted, which would mean a transfer to FBI headquarters in Quantico, Virginia. Carl was very good at his job, so I was sure it was just a matter of time before the promotion and transfer happened.

"Sebastien, how are you doing?" he said as he walked toward me.

"Good," I said. "CSI and the ME are still inside the kitchen. It's pretty ugly; not the same MO as Vegas, but every bit as sadistic. I'm sure it's the same killer."

"I called Vegas right after I got off the phone with you. Special Agent Gary Duval is en route, bringing two DHS agents with him. He lands at Eppley Airfield in less than two hours."

"I worked with him in Vegas. I actually just got back from there last night. I knew the first victim too."

Carl knew that Patsy and I were longtime friends. "Both victims were friends of yours? Sorry, Seb. That's rough."

I nodded.

"What's Duval like?"

"Very professional. He heads up the counterterrorism unit in Vegas, and he thinks our suspect is Daryl Parker, the ringleader of the ecoterrorism group Vegan National.

Personally, I am starting to believe the killer is a different person."

"What makes you say that?" Carl asked as we walked toward the entrance of the restaurant.

"We have two dead chefs who had very close ties through personal life and business. There was a third person involved in the same ventures. And I think he is in real danger. I am referring to Master Chef Pierre LeJeune, owner of Celadon, the famous restaurant in Chicago."

My call to Chef LeJeune was overdue, and I intended to remedy that as soon as I brought Carl into kitchen to view the crime scene.

Chapter 34

As Carl surveyed the crime scene I went into the dining room, pulled out my phone, and called Celadon. It might be too early for the master chef to be there, but I needed to warn him of the potential danger, so I wanted to make contact as soon as possible.

After the third ring a female voice said, "Thank you for calling Celadon. How may I help you?"

"Good morning. This is Detective Sebastien Saint-Gemmes of the Omaha Police Department. I am an acquaintance of Chef LeJeune. May I speak with him please? It is very important."

"Chef LeJeune is not here today, sir. He went fishing with a friend. My name is Victoria, and I am the general manager. May I help you, or can I relay a message to the chef?"

"I need to talk to him ASAP. He might be in danger," I said in a firm voice. I remained calm but communicated the urgency. "Do you have a number where I can reach him?"

"He is at his cabin. There is no phone there; it's in the middle of nowhere. The chef left his cell phone here, as he didn't want to be disturbed while fishing with his friend. He's due back tomorrow."

"All right. I need you to give me the address of the cabin, please," I said.

"I don't have it, sir. I can see if I can find a cell number for the friend who accompanied Chef LeJeune. If the gentleman has his phone with him perhaps we can reach them that way. I will call you back as soon as I find the number. Where can I reach you?" She seemed to finally realize that the situation was

169

actually serious.

"This is the best way to reach me," I said, giving her my cell number. "Please call me back when you have any information, Victoria."

"I will," she said.

"Thank you. As I said, it is extremely urgent that I speak with Chef LeJeune as soon as possible."

I ended the call and put my phone back in my pocket. Through the street-side windows, I stared at the chaos in the street. Two news vans were already parked and deploying their equipment. I knew it would be just a matter of minutes before I would have to address the media. KETV and Channel 6 News had their main field anchors on the story, hungry for some potential national news. Unfortunately, every murder in town was a top story to them, especially one connected to the high-profile case in Las Vegas.

My phone rang, and I saw on the green screen of my device that it was Ben Oswald calling me back—hopefully, to give me some good news.

"Ben, what do you have for me?" I asked impatiently.

"Pressure is on, I guess," he said, quickly moving on to the main subject. "I compiled an electronic file for you to check for yourself. There was a lot of activity straight through to 2:00 a.m., when the bars closed. After that, we have less movement, with the last drunks leaving and staff from the various bars going to their cars. At 3:00 a.m. everything is definitely quieter, and it stays that way for about two hours. At 5:00 a.m. the activity picks up again. I'm not really sure what I'm looking for specifically. I'm sending it to you right now. You'll have it on your phone in a minute."

"Thank you very much, Ben. Please run the video in slow motion to check the activity between 5:00 a.m. and 7:00 a.m., in the vicinity of the restaurant. Get back to me if you have anything. This is the number-one priority right now."

"Will do."

I ended the call, waited a few seconds for the file to come through, and selected Download to store it on my phone. I then decided to go to the Drunken Frog. I could view the video and fill Moose in on what had happened, all at the same time.

Randy Lewis and Carl Bruni were talking outside La Cigale when I interrupted them to let them know of my plans and where I was going.

I walked a block west, and when I arrived Moose was standing outside watching the show.

"Rough morning already," he said.

"Yes. Patsy Williams is dead, Moose. She was murdered this morning."

"What! You're kidding me! Who would want to kill Patsy? She is such a nice lady." Tears filled Moose's eyes.

In the restaurant industry, we were all so close that the bond between us created a sense of family. A member of the family was gone now. I understood the scope of Moose's grief, and I shared it.

"I need to check the street surveillance video," I told Moose. "I'm going to sit at the bar and get a coffee."

Moose opened the front door and we both entered the large space. The restaurant was completely empty and quiet. It was almost unreal and certainly peaceful. I liked the feeling when the staff sat down at the bar at the end of the night after all the customers had gone, and the place was finally ours again for a few minutes. No music, no kitchen chaos, no background noise—just the conversation of the waiters, bussers and cooks.

It was really quiet this morning in this old red-brick building, as nobody was working in the front area. Some cooks were already working in the kitchen, preparing some confit and sausage. I identified the prep by smell, but I didn't hear a thing. I figured it was going to be a busy lunch service today and ongoing, as La Cigale would likely be closed indefinitely. All the press, law enforcement and curious citizens would camp out in this part of downtown for a while. It was a sad moment. Getting extra business as a result of the death of your competitor was sobering indeed—especially when that competitor was also your close friend.

As I waited for the video files to download, Moose brought me a fresh-brewed cup of coffee.

"Thanks, man, I need this," I said as I took a sip.

"I still can't believe it, Seb!" he said.

"I know. We will miss her."

Files organized chronologically appeared on my screen, waiting to be opened. I hoped to finally catch a glimpse of our killer. We really needed a break in this case.

Although I'd been in the restaurant with Patsy during the midnight hour, I opened the file that showed the street views from 12:01 a.m. to 1:00 a.m.

Slowly the image appeared on my screen; activity in the streets appeared normal, with a fair amount of foot traffic along the sidewalks. Soon the amount of people in the street began to thin out. I had access to four different cameras, and all of them had short-angle views to the alley in the back of the restaurant, and also to the street in front of the restaurant. I found nothing in the first two to three hours of footage. By around 2:30 a.m. the streets of downtown were pretty empty. The remaining bar staff and the late-night revelers all were leaving, either in cabs or their own cars, headed home. It was pretty much exactly what Ben had told me over the phone.

I stretched before opening the next file.

My phone rang, so I switched to the main screen and saw the medical examiner's number.

"What do you have for me, Roger?"

"Time of death was at around 6:00 a.m. I'll call you with my findings after I complete the autopsy. If I find anything noteworthy during the autopsy, I'll let you know."

"Thank you, Roger."

Flipping back to the files, I decided to fast-forward to see what I could find from 5:00 a.m. onward. Nothing unusual at first. A few trucks driving up and down the streets. The Omaha World Herald van stopped in front of a newsstand to drop off the daily papers; a Scooter Coffee vehicle delivered freshly roasted beans and fresh pastries. Nobody stopped at La Cigale. Another twenty minutes of footage elapsed, and then, all of a sudden, some quick movement caught my attention, disappearing almost instantaneously. At first I thought I was seeing things. But then I looked again, and sure enough, there was a shadow at the bottom left corner of my screen. The camera providing the view was located in the alley behind La Cigale, where the employee/service door and garbage bin were located. I slowly rewound the digital images, and then I enlarged the image in question to full-screen.

"Right there!" I shouted at the screen.

"What did you see?" Moose asked, running over to where I sat at the bar.

"Right there—look. It's very fast, but you can clearly see that someone's hiding between the garbage bin and the outside wall at the back of the restaurant." I traced the shadowy movement with my finger, letting it hover just above the screen. "I need to get this image clarified as soon as possible. See you later ... have a good day, Moose."

"Gonna try, man. You too," Moose called after me.

I left the Drunken Frog and walked back to La Cigale at a brisk pace, wanting to give Randy and Carl the update face-to-face.

This might just be the break we'd been waiting for...

Chapter 35

Randy and Carl stood in front of La Cigale talking. The street was still very active, with a constant ballet of fire trucks, ambulances and patrol cars, but all the sirens had come to a halt.

"Chief!" I called out, interrupting their conversation. "I am sorry to cut you off, gentlemen, but I think I have a potential breakthrough. I went through the street video surveillance and found an image of someone hiding by the service door of the restaurant. I just need to ask Ben Oswald to work on enhancing the image so that we can get a better look at the face."

"Great! Everyone knows this is priority one. Let Ben know right away," Randy said.

"On it, Boss," I told him.

"Send me a copy as well," Carl said. "I can have my tech work on it at the Omaha field office." He pulled out his phone to call his office.

"No problem," I said.

I called Ben to ask him to enlarge the image, giving him the file specs so he would know where to look. I then e-mailed the file to Carl so he could send it to his tech.

In the meantime, Randy had told the CSI team to go to the alley behind the restaurant, and I walked to meet them there. J. J. and the rest of the team led the way in their full CSI gear, instructing everyone else to stay back in order to avoid contaminating the crime scene.

We watched them, and I tried to be patient.

After a few minutes, my phone rang. I saw Erica's number come up on my screen.

"Hi, Sebastien," Erica said, after I pushed Talk on my

phone.

"Good morning, young lady. How are you this morning?" I said. "Thanks for calling me back. I'm amazed; the connection is bright and clear, just as if you were right next to me."

"That's because I am here, not too far from you."

I turned around, and to my surprise, there was Erica just a few feet away from me. Behind her were Special Agent Gary Duval and three other suits.

"Good to see you again, Detective," Agent Duval said as he extended his hand.

Shaking his hand, I said, "Welcome to Omaha." I then scanned the men behind him.

"This is Agent Steve Donahue from the Las Vegas field office; these two gentlemen are Agents Pierce and Banks from DHS. You already know Detective Hunter. We decided to bring her along, as she is our LVMPD liaison. Tell us what you have."

We all stood in the alley while CSI dusted for prints and bagged evidence. I explained to the group from Las Vegas what had been going on in Omaha for the past four hours, including the potential lead I'd discovered on the video surveillance of the street.

They listened carefully. After a time, they each went in different directions in order to get a better understanding of the situation and location.

I told Erica that I would meet her later, and then I excused myself. I wanted to go back to the Drunken Frog, where I knew I would find the quiet and peace of mind I needed in order to concentrate on the investigation.

I was still waiting to receive a call that would provide me with Master Chef LeJeune's cabin address, or a viable cell number, but I had heard nothing so far. The Miami detective provided no pertinent information beyond what Elizabeth Dewey had already told me, so while waiting for the other calls to come through, I decided to call the Florida attorney she'd mentioned. I needed to obtain as much information as I could regarding the lawsuit and bankruptcy following the closure of Above the Stars.

A soft female voice answered after two rings. "Office of Norwalk and James, Attorneys-at-Law."

"Hello. This is Detective Saint-Gemmes from the Omaha Police Department. May I speak to Mr. Harold James, please?"

"Mr. James is not in right now. Would you like to leave a message?"

"Yes, please," I replied. "Do you know when he will be back in the office? This is an urgent matter."

"He should be back late this afternoon or first thing in the morning. Please hold, and I'll put you through to voice mail. He checks it while he's out of the office."

I thanked her, waited for his message and then said into the phone, "Mr. James, this is Detective Sebastien Saint-Gemmes of the Omaha Police Department, and I need to talk to you right away concerning the lawsuit and bankruptcy related to the restaurant Above the Stars, and its owners. Elizabeth Dewey gave me your name and contact information. Please call me as soon as possible. It is extremely urgent." After leaving all the phone numbers where he could reach me, I ended the call.

I put my phone away, starting to feel uneasy about the whole situation. We were running out of time to stop what my gut told me would be the next murder.

****

After more than half an hour Erica called me, and I gave her directions to the Drunken Frog from La Cigale. She and Special Agent Duval entered my restaurant and joined me at the bar. We all sat at the beautiful U-shaped mahogany bar, with the whole restaurant in full view. Bottles of wine were located in a corner to the left of the entrance, in a two-story glass tower. The temperature-controlled room kept all the wine at the perfect temperature. Owning a restaurant was hard work, but it had its perks, the main one being the great access to a lot of varieties of wine. The first tier of the tower was divided into two sections: French and American. These were the wines we had the most of, and our wine list was organized in geographical sections. The second tier held wines from the rest of the world, and also included our reserve liquor. The back bar was filled with all the high-end vodka, single malt whisky, rum and more. A hidden light located behind the wood gave the bottles a look of drama and mystery. The whole atmosphere made the inside of the restaurant warm and inviting.

I watched Erica and Agent Duval take it all in, and then I invited them to sit at the bar, giving them each a glass of water.

Agent Duval immediately asked me about the connection between Chefs Bob Dewey and Patsy Williams.

"I spoke with Patsy at length last night and was planning to meet with her again this morning. She was supposed to give me more information on the lawsuit resulting from the death of two children infected with E. coli during an outbreak at Above the Stars, the restaurant she and Chefs Dewey and LeJeune had in the King Arthur in Las Vegas. I have not seen the paperwork, so I cannot provide any details. She said she would bring the documents pertaining to the lawsuit with her this morning, but the search of her office turned up nothing."

"Chef LeJeune was not in any of the pictures in the Vegan National building back in Las Vegas, but his name keeps coming up in our investigation," Erica said.

"Yes," I said. "We need to get a hold of him as soon as possible. I left a message at his restaurant in Chicago. He is out of town and unreachable at the moment." I paused and then added, "All the evidence seems to point to him as the potential third victim."

My phone rang in my pocket, interrupting our conversation. Excusing myself, I answered it.

"Detective Saint-Gemmes speaking."

"Hello, Detective. This is Harold James returning your call."

"Mr. James, thank you for returning my call. Hold on; let me put you on speaker." After pressing the appropriate buttons I continued. "Mr. James, you are on speaker with Special Agent Gary Duval of the FBI, Las Vegas office and Detective Erica Hunter of the Las Vegas Metropolitan Police Department. We are working on a case involving two murders: one in Las Vegas, and one here in Omaha. It is my understanding from Elizabeth Dewey that you represented Chef Bob Dewey and Chef Patsy Williams in a lawsuit resulting from two food-related deaths at the Above the Stars restaurant in the King Arthur Hotel and Casino in Las Vegas some years ago. Is that correct?"

"Yes, it is. May I ask why you contacted me?"

"The victims in our murder case are Chefs Dewey and Williams; they both were murdered in the past few days, and we would like to know who else was involved in the lawsuit."

"Oh my God. I am so sorry to hear that they were killed. If memory serves, Chef LeJeune in Chicago was the third party in the lawsuit."

"That confirms our theory," I said as I looked at my two companions. "One more question, Mr. James. Who issued the lawsuit?"

"Well, the plaintiffs were not in the United States. To my surprise, one was from Germany, and the other was from France."

"I need you to send me all your files on the lawsuit, please," I said.

"Well, it is confidential. I don't mind in this case, but I need an official request to cover my butt."

"You will have a formal request from the FBI in thirty

minutes," Agent Duval said. "Thank you for your cooperation."

We said good-bye and ended the call.

Agent Duval, Erica and I looked at one another.

"We need to find Chef LeJeune *now,* or he will be a dead man," I said.

Chapter 36

The FBI team searched La Cigale from top to bottom, looking for the paperwork related to the Above the Stars lawsuit, but like OPD, CSI did not find anything. A special warrant had been issued to search Patsy's house as well, but nothing turned up there either, even after hours of searching. Her office and home computers were taken to the FBI Omaha field office so that the tech team there could check all the files. We all hoped this would lead to a concrete lead on our killer.

The day went by pretty quickly, but without any breakthrough. We waited impatiently for an enlargement of the image from the video surveillance view of the back alley. And, I had not yet heard back on how to reach Chef LeJeune.

FBI Agent Carl Bruni and his team ran a mobile office from an SUV parked in front of La Cigale, and Special Agent Gary Duval had made it the central HQ for the murder investigation.

Before leaving the scene Chief Randy Lewis told me to work through them, letting Duval know that all of OPD's resources were at the FBI's disposal.

The ambulances and fire trucks were gone now, and just a few agents and police officers remained, going in and out of the restaurant.

By five o'clock the downtown streets were almost empty, except for the news vans. The media presence had not died down; their big satellite dishes were in place, and all the news anchors sat around, waiting to go live for the six o'clock news. Yellow tape still blocked the crime scene, both the facing and back streets. Some pedestrians seemed curious, but most had lost interest, given the lack of action on the street. Plus, the murder was headline news on every TV and computer screen in and around Omaha, so there was more to see via the media outlet of choice than at the actual location. Dinner customers seemed to be staying away, whether spooked by the violent crime or simply seeking to avoid downtown because of the street closures and lack of parking.

I knew that business for the night was pretty much shot. Moose had already given all but a few servers and cooks the night off; he texted me to say he was planning on an early closing.

At 5:30 p.m. my phone rang, showing the number for my cousin Michel in France.

"Salut, cousin!" I said. "Not in bed yet?"

He responded to my English by using English too. "Hey, Seb. No, not in bed yet. How are you doing?"

"Good. How about you? Still working past midnight?"

"Married to my job, just like you." He laughed. "What can I do for you?"

"Well, two of my chef friends were murdered here in the states. It looks like it may have something to do with an arrest Interpol made in Germany. Friedrich Heinz of Munich. Can you please find some more information on it for me? This case is getting crazier and crazier. We might be dealing with ecoterrorism, but then again, it might just be simple revenge."

"Hah! You have been in America too long, Seb. Revenge is never simple."

"You are right about that. Thank you, Michel. Call me when you get something."

"Will do, cousin. Say hi to Marie and Tom for me."

"Same. Kisses to Uncle Giovanni and Aunt Celina."

We said our good-byes, and I put my phone away for the moment.

An hour or so later one of the calls I'd been waiting for all day finally arrived. I answered as soon as I saw Ben Oswald's number.

"Hey, Seb. It's Ben," he said. "I have your guy. The image is not 100 percent clear, but I think we can work with that. I'm sending it to you now; you'll have it on your phone in a few seconds."

"Great job, Ben! Thanks. Talk to you soon."

Five seconds after I ended the call, my phone beeped to signal the receipt of a message. I opened the message, clicked on the attached image, and the killer of two of my friends appeared on my screen. It was a grainy image, but the man appeared to be tall and physically fit, with what looked like dark hair lined with some gray.

"I got the image!" I said to Erica and Agent Duval, both of whom were with me in the restaurant. "I'm sending it now; you should have it on your phones in a second."

The image of the killer was etched in my mind.

"Got it," said Agent Duval. "Let's get this image everywhere we can. We have his face. Now we need to find out his name, even an alias. The suspect was here very early this morning; he may have stayed in a hotel downtown or across the river in Council Bluffs, maybe at one of the casinos." He started tapping away on his phone, and then added, "I will send this image to FBI headquarters and all field offices, telling Des Moines and Chicago to be on high alert."

"I'll check in with LVMPD, see if anything new has come up," Erica said.

Agent Duval nodded as he walked out of the restaurant, headed toward his mobile HQ.

"I'm going to call my boss to ask him to distribute the image to all patrols; they can ask questions around downtown."

"Sounds like a plan," Erica said.

"Okay. Excuse me for the moment," I said, but then I turned around. "Dinner together tonight?" I asked.

"Sure thing," she replied with a smile. "I thought you'd

never ask. Not too late, though; I believe tomorrow will be a long day."

"Sounds like a plan," I said, repeating her earlier response.

She smiled, and I winked at her.

I then forwarded the image to Randy, and as soon as it appeared in my Sent folder I called him.

Chapter 37

After a five-hour drive the Handler arrived in Davenport, Iowa, right after lunch. He stopped at the last gas station on I-80, and then got on Highway 61, headed north toward DeWitt. The cabin of target number three was located right on the Wapsinicon River, on a two hundred-acre parcel of land. He had spied on Master Chef Pierre LeJeune a year ago, so he knew the fishing and hunting habits of the chef and his friend. There were only two of them at the cabin, and after a day outdoors they would cook their catches and drink wine at the table on the patio.

The Handler parked his rental car in front of a bar located in the tiny town of McCausland, known to be a hunting departure point because of its proximity to the river, the woods and the land. Nobody would pay any attention to just another out-of-town visitor there to hunt or fish. He loaded his backpack, took his rifle and headed toward the woods. After an hour of walking through the woods, he arrived at the boundary of Chef LeJeune's property. He opened his bag, checked the property specs he'd obtained and smiled. His destination was close at hand. He rested for a bit, hidden behind some trees, and waited for dusk to descend.

At around 5:00 p.m. it was almost completely dark in the woods. The Handler put on his night-vision goggles, picked up his bag and rifle and started to walk toward the cabin at a regular pace. He could see the two men smoking cigars on the front porc'h, just a few hundred yards away from him; they were laughing hard, enjoying the moment. After finding a flat spot where he could lie down and take position, facing the front of the house, he removed his night goggles and adjusted the silencer on his weapon. Thanks to an advanced night scope, he could almost see the brand of cigars they were smoking. After loading six bullets he paused to analyze the situation. Two targets, six bullets; he knew he was not the best sniper in the world, but he'd had great training during his time in the army. He had enough bullets to do the job.

He breathed in silence for a few seconds, feeling his body relax. His heartbeat slowed to the perfect rate. He was in a mode of pure concentration and focus.

He would follow his original plan: shoot the chef first, and then his friend.

Into the night two pops sounded, muffled by the silencer. After that, total silence filled the surrounding space. One man lay on the porch; the other sat in his rocking chair, still moving a bit, with his head tilted back. After a moment the movements ceased.

The nocturnal creatures of the woods continued their lives as usual; the two dead men on the porch were of no consequence.

The Handler remained where he was for a few minutes, continuing to look through the scope to make sure there was no movement. Nothing. It seemed that two bullets were sufficient for the job.

"Thank you, US Army, for the training," he said in a barely audible whisper.

He then packed all his goods back in the bag, picked up the rifle and walked toward the cabin. The job was not yet finished. The Mastermind had requested special "extras" on all the jobs.

Two hours later the Handler was back in his rental car, en route to the airport. His plane was scheduled to depart at 11:00 p.m.

Chapter 38

I picked up my phone after the first ring. "Detective Saint-Gemmes."

"Hello, Detective, this is Victoria at Celadon in Chicago. You called earlier, looking for Chef LeJeune."

"Yes, I did. Have you heard from him? Or have you found a number where I can reach him? It is very urgent for me to get in contact with him, as I explained to you earlier. He might be in danger."

"I double-checked everywhere, Detective, but I couldn't find an address for the cabin. I was able to check Chef LeJeune's cell phone to find his friend's number. I called the number, but there was no answer. It might just be because reception is poor in that remote area. I am so sorry, Detective; I did try. May I ask why it is so urgent, and what the danger is?"

"It is confidential information right now. Please give me the make and model of Chef LeJeune's car. I also need his friend's cell number."

After getting all the info, I ended the call and immediately contacted Carl. He said the FBI would try to triangulate the phone to find the location of the two men, and also see if the chef's car had a chip locator that could be tracked.

Time was running out; it was already 7:00 p.m.

A few minutes later the Iowa State Patrol called to inform me that nothing seemed out of the ordinary on the highways of the Hawkeye State.

Was I wrong to assume Chef LeJeune would be the next target? This self-doubt went out of my mind as fast as it came in. I knew I was right. I was sure that we were far from the Vegan National terrorist theory, and I felt confident that my suspicion of personal revenge in response to the food-related deaths at Above the Stars was the motive behind these murders. No paperwork on the lawsuits had been uncovered. We were still waiting on a callback from Harold James, the attorney who had represented Chefs Dewey, Williams and LeJeune in the lawsuit that resulted from the E. coli outbreak. So, we were pretty much in limbo.

Erica's voice interrupted my thoughts. "How are you feeling, Seb?" she asked.

I turned around, happy to see her smiling face. It felt good to see her standing in front of me. She was so beautiful.

"Rough day so far," I said. "Frustrating. I hate waiting for people to call back when time is so short."

"I understand," she said, putting her hand on my shoulder.

"Are you getting hungry?" I asked, realizing when my stomach growled that I had not eaten all day.

"Yes, I could use something."

"Great! Let's go to my restaurant. Moose will take good care of us."

We walked the block to the Drunken Frog.

Moose greeted us at the door. I introduced my two friends to each other, and Moose welcomed Erica with open arms.

"Welcome to our gastro pub!" he said as he directed us to the bar.

"It's such a beautiful place!" Erica said, more for Moose's benefit than mine; she hadn't had a chance to meet or talk to him when she and Agent Duval were at the bar with me earlier in the day.

We sat down at the bar.

Eugene, the bartender, greeted us. He offered us some

water, gave us the menus and told us about the specials for the evening: seared Nebraska ostrich served with blueberry gastrique, quinoa cake and fresh vegetables, and fresh seared and oven-baked monkfish, flown from the East Coast this morning, served with a Truebridge Farm bacon-cream sauce, polenta and grilled asparagus."

"I will have the fish special, please," I said to Eugene.

"I will have the ostrich," Erica said. "I never had that bird before." She flashed a smile that showed hesitation but also interest in trying something new.

"Great choices," Eugene said. "Seb, what do you want to drink with that?"

"Give us a Pinot Noir from Alsace, please. Thanks, Eugene."

Eugene put our order in to the kitchen, got the wine and decanted it.

Erica and I talked for a bit, while letting the wine breathe. After a few minutes I motioned for Moose to join us for a drink.

"To Patsy and Bob!" I said as I raised my glass.

"To Patsy and Bob!" they echoed.

The three of us toasted, and then we each took a sip of this amazing fresh Pinot served in the thin and elegant green-stemmed glasses typical of Alsace, the French region near the German border. It was the only area in France where wines were described by the grape and not the name of the vineyard. Contrary to the Bordeaux region which divided its wines into sub-areas like Saint-Estèphe, Margaux, or Pommerol, with some specific grape in each one of them; the Alsatian wines were known right off the bat for their grape names: Gewürztraminer, Sylvaner, Riesling, Pinot Blanc, Pinot Gris and only Pinot Noir for the reds. I fell in love with this fresh red liquid at a restaurant in Paris, Le Congres on Place Maillot. Seafood was the house specialty, and I had gone there with my parents during a visit back to France. They served enormous seafood trays filled with oysters, mussels, scallops, shrimp, crab and lobster, all of it served with rye bread and salted butter. And, the Pinot Noir complemented it perfectly. I'd tried to replicate the dish at the Drunken Frog, but it did not fit the local tastes.

Moose talked to Erica while I mused on the delicacies of Paris and Alsace, and then he excused himself after finishing his glass of wine.

Our dinners were served promptly, and we enjoyed our meal, talking about everything except the case. Erica found learning about Alsatian wine and Parisian seafood fascinating, and I relished the opportunity to show off. As in Vegas, we both needed to distract ourselves from the stress of the gruesome case.

We also talked to Eugene and the rest of the crew, all of them eager to meet Erica, who was the first "real date" I'd brought to the restaurant in a while.

"I really love this place, Seb. And Moose is great." She smiled. "The food was amazing; I did not expect the ostrich to be a red meat. It was wonderful—very lean and so tasty. I will order it again."

"Well, thank you for the compliment." I turned to Moose, who had come up to the bar again while Eugene took a short break. "Please, pass that along to the kitchen."

"Will do," he said, nodding graciously to Erica as he finished pouring the rest of the wine into our glasses.

"Any dessert?" I asked Erica. "We have an amazing pastry chef who works wonders in the back. We are well known for our strawberry opera and our triple chocolate mousse."

At that point I felt Erica's hand on my leg. I looked down and then raised my eyes to meet hers.

"I want to have dessert at your place." Her tone was so erotic that I almost melted right in front of her.

"My place? You know we can be disturbed at any time

of the night to go back on the case."

"I realize that, so let's not lose any time." She moved her hand up, squeezing the inside of my thigh.

On that note, I left a forty-dollar tip on the bar, did my reverence to the staff and walked out to my car with Erica, headed toward my home in the Westside suburb.

Chapter 39

In the middle of the night my phone rang. I looked over at it. The screen showed that it was 3:30 a.m., and my boss was providing the wake-up call. I surmised it was the phone call we'd been expecting.

"Saint-Gemmes?" said my boss on the other end of the line.

"Yes, sir," I said, sitting up and swinging my legs over the side of my king-size bed.

"I am with Agents Duval and Bruni. We triangulated the cell phone of Chef LeJeune's friend, and it is located in eastern Iowa, in the middle of the forest close to the Wapsipinicon River, at the border of Illinois. There's a plane leaving Eppley in one hour. Contact Detective Hunter; you both need to be on that plane."

Erica was up and out of bed as soon as I answered the phone. By the time I ended the call, she was in the bathroom.

"We have to get to the airport. There's a plane leaving in one hour," I told her through the closed door.

"No problem. I will be out in two minutes."

I chuckled to myself while I got dressed. Didn't women usually need at least half an hour to get ready? Well, not in this case. Erica came out of the bathroom with the same smile she'd had when we left the restaurant.

"You look amazing, even with just a few hours' sleep," I said, grabbing her by the waist to kiss her. "Last night was amazing; I truly enjoyed my dessert. I need to talk to Moose about adding it to the menu." I winked and smiled at her.

"Let's get in the car. We can talk on the way to the

airport," she said, squeezing my bottom.

An hour after Randy's call we were aboard an FBI private plane, headed for Davenport, Iowa. The local authorities were already on their way to Chef LeJeune's cabin. A helicopter from the FBI field office was waiting for us at the airfield. We would soon find out if we were too late.

Chapter 40

We landed in Davenport, Iowa after only thirty minutes in the air. As promised, just fifty yards from the plane a Black Hawk helicopter waited for us on the tarmac, with its rotors going full speed. Agents Duval and Donahue from Vegas boarded first; Carl, my friend and FBI contact in Omaha, boarded next; and Erica and I boarded last. The chopper then roared upward into the sky. Headphones muffled the noise somewhat.

The pilot's voice came through the headphones, letting us know that we would land in the vicinity of the cabin in approximately eight minutes. Local law enforcement—police and sheriff's department—had already headed for the cabin on foot, as it was impossible to reach the location by car or even ATV.

It was still dark outside, but a trace of the sunrise was slowly appearing on the horizon. Ten minutes later, we were walking toward the cabin, weapons drawn.

The sheriff's advanced team, which had been waiting for us for fifteen minutes, welcomed us as we approached, informing us that no noise was coming from the house but the lights were still on inside.

Agent Duval started giving directions to everyone.

Just then, I felt my phone vibrate in my pocket. Who could possibly be calling me at this hour? It wasn't even 5:30 a.m.; it had to be my boss or my cousin.

I motioned to Duval that I had to check an incoming call, looking at the screen to see that it was Michel's number. "My cousin at Interpol," I said.

Agent Duval nodded for me to take it, and then he

continued giving directions to the others.

"Hello?" I said into the phone, keeping my voice low.

"Hi, cousin. Am I waking you up?"

"No," I said. "We're on the verge of raiding a cabin in the middle of the woods, either to apprehend a suspect or discover more bodies. What's up?"

"Well, you asked me to check on a possible link between your case and that German guy, Friedrich Heinz. Interpol in Germany talked to our guy at his house. He is still pissed off at your victims, even if he had no idea two of the three chefs were dead. I don't believe he had anything to do with the murders. But, during the conversation, he mentioned a French guy whose daughter died as a result of the incident at the restaurant in Las Vegas. This guy lives in southwestern France. Heinz did not remember the name, but I am looking into it. I will call you back as soon as I have more info."

"Thanks, cousin! I owe you one," I said, ending the call and putting my phone back in my pocket.

Agent Duval was looking at me. "Any info that can be useful?" he asked.

"I believe so. I have had some doubts about the Vegan National terrorist group being responsible for the murders. I called my cousin Michel, who is the head of Interpol in Paris. They interviewed someone involved in the lawsuit against our victims. He mentioned someone else who may be a person of interest: a French guy whose daughter died as a result of the incident. That would definitely be a good reason to seek revenge."

"Interesting," said Duval. "We'll talk about it later. For now, let's get to the cabin. Detectives, stay by me."

After putting on bulletproof vests and checking our weapons, we started to walk slowly into the sunrise.

The cabin was already surrounded by police and sheriff's deputies. The three FBI agents, Erica and I walked toward the house at the same pace. We approached the entrance of the house. Agent Duval directed Carl to join the sheriff's deputies on the left, while he had Agent Donahue go to the right, with the police in SWAT gear. Erica and I followed Agent Duval straight ahead.

As we approached the front porch I saw two splatters of blood on the outside wall beside the front door. Chunks of what seemed to be brain matter covered the outside wall as well. Two rocking chairs moved in the light wind, as did the wind chime; it sounded sharp in the early morning stillness.

Everything was quiet, which was not good news.

Agent Duval went up the stairs and reached the front door; Erica and I followed. The floor creaked a little under our weight as we walked. The cabin seemed pretty new to my eyes. Blood on the floor to my left told me the victim was shot while sitting in the chair and then fell from it. As for the right chair, it looked like blood had dripped horizontally, meaning the second victim had been shot there but did not move afterward. Large amounts of blood traces led inside the house. A strange garlic smell wafted from the cabin.

At Agent Duval's go-ahead, each segment of the team rushed inside the cabin at once. The house was fairly small: what appeared to be two bedrooms and a large living room. As we entered the space, a thick fog enveloped us, and a strong odor of boiled chicken came to our nostrils. After a few seconds the cloud dissipated, and we all quickly realized the reason for the noxious cloud.

In the next second we ran out of the cabin, gasping and retching in response to the horror we had just encountered.

Chapter 41

No one vomited, but we all did have to take large gulps of air once we were out of the cabin.

The crime scene we had just discovered was one of the most horrific I had ever experienced; as bad as the one inside La Cigale yesterday, if not worse. I wondered who could be sick enough to do that to another human being.

After a few minutes Agent Duval and I went back inside. The cloud, which was actually steam, had fully dissipated, but the Jacuzzi was still running and the motor made loud popping sounds.

I walked toward the electrical panel, the screen of which flashed 212°F: the boiling point. I quickly shut off the power and a sense of calm finally descended upon the room.

Human remains floated on the surface of the water in the tub. Once again, each joint had been broken; and in this case, sawed into pieces. The flesh was a brownish color, and the bare skin seemed to be swollen. A thin layer of bright-yellow fat coated the water, and some areas of the mutilated body had a gelatinous look. Some of the bare bones revealed retracted flesh where the marrow had melted. In places the skin had a reddish tint, indicating the use of salt in the water. I turned around, and right beside the Jacuzzi there was an empty box of kosher salt, taken from La Cigale, no doubt. The remnants of what appeared to be garlic cloves and black peppercorns floated on the water.

The Jacuzzi had to have been running for a few hours in order to achieve this final horror. I checked the electrical panel to see if it had been tampered with so that it would reach 212 degrees Fahrenheit.

Carl found the second body in a bedroom closet. The victim had been shot in the head and still had his fishing clothes on. I looked at the corpse in the bedroom but didn't recognize him, so I concluded it was Chef LeJeune's remains that we had found in the Jacuzzi. The effects of the boiling water rendered him unrecognizable. I knew we needed an autopsy to confirm that it was he, but I had no doubt.

In that moment, everything started to make sense.

"All the murders are connected to food," I said, loud enough for everyone to hear me. No one responded, but I continued to explain my theory. "My explanation might not be pleasant to hear, but what I am going to tell you reflects the truth about food production as it still occurs today, in many cases, and as it was done in the past. All the murders have staged phases of cooking preparation and techniques, at least to some extent. Chef Bob Dewey in Las Vegas, the first victim, showed the technique of preparing duck, emphasizing that the birds are force-fed corn mash to enrich their livers. It is actually a gastronomical delicacy that has existed for centuries in Europe. The murderer stuffed a mixture of corn and water down Chef Bob Dewey's throat, suffocating him. He died of asphyxia, which does not happen to the ducks, by the way."

Everybody was looking at me now, trying to make sense of my culinary jargon.

"Go on, Saint-Gemmes," said Agent Duval.

"Chef Patsy Williams's throat was cut, just as we do to many animals in order to bleed them before preparing them for cutting. The salt is used to preserve the meat. It was the main method used in the past to prevent the rotting of animal flesh. Meat and fish were conserved in barrels in this manner, and they could last months that way, even years. It is also a technique used to make duck confit, a delicacy of southwestern France, in which the ducks' hindquarters are rubbed with sea salt for flavor."

The mouths of half my audience dropped as they listened to my explanation of food production. I was not surprised. Many supermarket customers and restaurant patrons had no clue as to how food was actually prepared. Most of them actually had no desire to know how the production line worked. All they wanted was a tenderloin or a chicken breast. They wanted to be able to cook their meat without thinking about the process of how it got to the place of purchase. Most people were happy to have a fried fish square on their plates; they didn't want to see the head and the fins.

"Our third victim, whom I assume is Master Chef Pierre LeJeune, represents the final result of the production. For many centuries, boiling water has been the means for cooking food. Unfortunately, we can see that our victim received the same method of treatment. Chef LeJeune was literally boiled in the same way you cook a chicken purchased at your local supermarket. The process is the same. In this case, because of the salt, garlic and peppercorns, I believe the intention was to replicate the recipe for cooking duck. Instead of using duck fat, which would have been too difficult to find in big quantity, our killer just used the water. This is the way you prepare the duck confit delicacy I mentioned earlier. You submerge the duck legs in duck fat, add salt, peppercorns and garlic; and then, you cook it at a very low temperature until the meat falls off the bone. It is delicious, I assure you."

Seeing their horrified expressions, I realized I should not have added that last part. I was accustomed to having my culinary and detective work side by side, but my colleagues were not.

One of the local police officers said, "Wow! All that is going to make me think twice about the food I eat."

Agent Duval stepped toward me. "Saint-Gemmes, tell me more about this duck dish. What did you call it again?"

"Duck confit," I said. "It is actually the duck thigh and leg, cooked in its own fat. It is most often used in cassoulet, a kind of stew. These are specialties of southwestern France."

Erica said, "It looks like everything is pointing to that region in France, and interestingly enough, some of the lawsuits came from Europe. I don't believe it is a coincidence. I think we can stop looking at the Vegan National terrorist group; we should focus on the French lead instead."

"I believe so," I said. "My cousin, who called me just before we raided the cabin, is the head of Interpol in Paris. His team is tracking some individuals involved in the lawsuit against the three dead chefs."

We exited the cabin and settled ourselves outside. The sun lit up the beautiful blue sky, and we could finally see the amazingly peaceful surroundings of the cabin. The brutal crimes committed inside were in stark contrast to the pristine serenity outside.

A helicopter ambulance was on its way, with a CSI team to take care of the corpse and what was left of the poor chef.

After checking the entire property, Agent Donahue found the spot where the shots had been fired, and he set up a perimeter with yellow crime-scene tape.

By 1:00 p.m. all we had was my food theory as the MO, and a potential location. It was pretty slim but better than what we'd had up to now.

After seeing the horror in the Jacuzzi, I was more determined than ever to find the murderer. I would bring my friends' killer to justice—no matter what it took.

Chapter 42

I went for a walk along the river near the cabin, and while there I received a phone call from Harold James.

"Any news for us, Mr. James? We are still waiting for your files."

"I apologize, Detective. Our firm had considered the case closed, so all the files were archived. I'm having them pulled as we speak. Are there any updates in the case?"

"We just found the body of Chef LeJeune, which means all three chefs involved in the lawsuit have now been killed within days of one another. We are leaning toward potential suspects from Europe, especially from Germany and France, which jibes with the information you gave us the first time we spoke."

"Yes, it does. I should have the files in the next two hours, Detective. I'll call you as soon as I get them."

"Please do. Thank you for your cooperation. I will expect your call soon."

I heard the ambulance chopper fly overhead as I walked back to the cabin.

Agent Duval came toward me. There was a smile on his face as he held up his phone.

"What's new?" I asked.

"After talking about Europe, I decided to send the picture of our suspect to all the international airports in the Midwest—Chicago, Minneapolis, Detroit—to warn them of our murderer's possible attempt to leave the country. DHS in Chicago received an image of our suspect early this morning."

He showed me a clear image of our suspect on a TSA

photo. No doubt it was him.

"They're confirming that he boarded a plane last night, bound for Charles de Gaulle in Paris. Unfortunately, due to the delay in getting the photo out and the ahead-of-schedule arrival of the plane, the French police were too late to apprehend him. He is roaming the streets of the French capital."

I grimaced. Before I could respond, he put up his hand.

"I already talked to my director, Saint-Gemmes. You are leaving for France on the 6:00 p.m. flight from Chicago to Paris."

"I don't have my passport, and I don't have any extra clothes."

"By the time you get to O'Hare everything will be arranged, as will your arrival in Paris. Call your cousin, please, and get Interpol apprised of the situation. We don't have any jurisdiction over there, but you are a French citizen. It will be easier for you, with the language and your connections. Just keep me informed."

It seemed I was going to be able to honor my promise to catch my friends' killer after all.

Chapter 43

After saying good-bye to everybody—especially Erica—I boarded the FBI helicopter bound for O'Hare in Chicago. The chopper flight took just less than an hour, flying at 160 miles an hour. The helicopter landed in the private-jet section of the airport, welcomed by two men in black suits who got out of an SUV. They flashed their badges as I got into the van, sitting in the back. We sped to the terminal where the Air France plane was scheduled to take off at 6:05 p.m.

It was 5:46 p.m. according to my watch, and I was afraid I would miss my plane, but the two agents assured me that the plane would wait for me.

"There is a black gym bag next to you, Detective," the agent in the front passenger seat told me. "In it you will find the paperwork to allow you to go through security and board the plane without being stopped. A second document will serve as a temporary passport, substituting for your actual French passport. Also in the bag is a basic change of clothes and a shaving kit. Please give me your weapon. You cannot board the plane with it. The air marshal aboard the plane is aware of the situation."

I obeyed, giving them my gun and the two extra cartridges.

"Good luck," the driver said.

As the driver hit the brake, the agent in the passenger seat got out and opened the door for me. "Please follow me," he said.

Seconds later, we were joined by a DHS agent. We started to run through the back door of the airport.

My phone rang, and I picked it up without breaking stride. "Saint-Gemmes."

"Hello, Detective, this is Harold James calling from Florida. Are you okay?"

"Yes, I'm running through the airport on my way to catch a plane. What do you have for me?" I asked him, trying to regulate my breathing in between running and talking.

"My memory served me well. There was a plaintiff from Germany and a plaintiff from France. Both were families on vacation in Las Vegas during the time of the E. coli outbreak; both families had eaten in Above the Stars. Let me just be clear that many individuals from Europe and the states simply accepted the compensation offered, and then went on with their lives. These two European families were the exception. The German family, the Heinzes, had a pretty tragic situation: the wife and one of the sons became ill in Germany within a month or so of the Vegas trip; the son recovered fully, but the wife sustained permanent kidney damage and paralysis, and the husband insisted that both illnesses were the result of the E. coli, even though doctors in Germany could not establish any connection and there was no evidence that they had eaten the tainted meat."

"Yes, Mr. James, I am familiar with the story of the Heinzes. Interpol in Germany just re-interviewed Mr. Heinz and concluded he is not involved with the murders. He mentioned a gentleman in southwestern France whom we think might be a person of interest. Is that the other party you are referring to?"

"Yes, I believe so, Detective. The daughter of the French couple died a few months after the accident, and they never accepted any compensation. The husband categorically refused any type of settlement, saying that money would not bring back his daughter. His name is Charles Dumont."

I listened carefully, and when he finished I said, "Finally. We have a name. Thank you, Mr. James."

He wished me luck, and we said good-bye.

After ending the call and putting my phone away, I realized we were already in the departure hall of international flights. Radios in hand, the agents barked orders and electronic doors were opened for us. I had never boarded a plane so quickly in my life.

We arrived at the departure gate at exactly 6:00 p.m. The person in charge of closing the door behind me breathed an audible sigh of relief when she saw that I had arrived. The plane was not going to be late, so she had fulfilled her job of making sure the flight was on time.

"Good luck, Detective," the FBI agent said as I walked through the corridor to the plane.

"Thank you!" I called over my shoulder.

I was greeted by a good-looking flight attendant who indicated that my seat was 5A, a window seat in first class. Not bad! As soon as I clicked my seat belt, the plane started moving.

After an hour in the sky I started to relax, and the flight attendant served me champagne. That was the beauty of Air France: they served champagne to all guests, even in economy class.

The flight attendant indicated that I could use my phone if I needed to, so I called Michel in Paris, even if it was the middle of the night for him.

"Caravaggio speaking," he said in a sleepy voice.

"Michel, this is Seb. I am on an Air France flight from Chicago. I will land in Paris at 5:30 a.m. Can you pick me up, please?"

"Sure! Are you coming for your case?"

"Yes. Our suspect is in France. He landed this morning. The French border police received the information too late to stop him at the end of the flight. I think he is coming into the country to finalize his contract and get paid. I am sending you a photo of him taken by the airport cameras in O'Hare. Please forward it to all the police; we need to catch him before he disappears."

"All right. Will do as soon as you send it," he said.

As I sent him the photo, I said, "Also, I got another name from the lawyer who defended my chef friends; this man is the only one who actually lost a child. His name is Charles Dumont. Can you please inquire about it? Sorry to wake you up, cousin."

"Got your picture, Seb. It is 2:00 a.m. I will contact Interpol central headquarters in Lyon to get some help. Try to get some sleep."

"You too, cousin. And, thank you. See you soon."

On that, we ended the call.

Only one call to make before closing my eyes.

"Hi, Thomas! How was your day, my son? You will never guess where I am right now."

Chapter 44

The Handler loved the city of Paris. As he descended into the Métro station at Saint-Michel, near Notre-Dame de Paris, he wondered who could possibly not love Paris. He was always stunned by the beauty of the French Gothic architecture of this edifice, built over the course of almost a hundred years, from the mid-twelfth to the mid-thirteenth century. Tons of tourists from all over the world were packed in front of the cathedral, taking pictures or just praying.

The Handler now recalled visiting Notre-Dame more than a year ago, when he met with the Mastermind to plan his work. They had met at a café, sat on the terrace and talked for a long time, mostly about family. Impressed with the Mastermind's sincerity and touched by the sadness of his life, the Handler had agreed to the deal. He was happy to be back in Paris and to be able to tell the Mastermind that the plan had been executed without any problems.

The Handler stopped at his hotel on the Boulevard de Saint-Germain-des-Prés, took a quick shower and laid down to rest a few minutes. He quickly fell asleep. He was dreaming of shopping in France with his daughter when the phone woke him.

"How was your flight?" the Mastermind asked him.

"Very good, thank you. Always nice to travel in first class."

"You are making the news, even here in France. Have you watched the news lately? CNN and Fox News have named you 'the Butcher.'"

"Wow! I am impressed," the Handler said. He paused and then asked, "How is everything with you?"

"I feel better, as you have now done your job, but it will not bring back my daughter. I just want to be done with all of it. I reserved a TGV train ticket for you, first class, to meet me for your final payment. Check your phone for the info. I will talk to you later. Enjoy Paris for the next two days," the Mastermind said.

"See you soon," the Handler responded.

They ended the call, and the Handler put his phone down.

He picked up the remote, turned on the TV and channel surfed to CNN Europe, staying there for a little while. There was nothing about him on the broadcast, so he turned off the TV.

He was wide awake now, and decided to spend the whole day walking the streets of the city. It was too late to call his daughter, because of the time difference, so he made a note to call her later when she would be awake.

A sense of happiness filled the Handler as he walked out of the hotel and stepped onto the sidewalk. The air was fresh, the sky was a crisp blue and the people in the street had smiles on their faces. He decided to walk up the Boulevard de Saint-Germain-des-Prés and stop at Café de Flore for a café au lait. He sat down at a table on the terrace, relaxing and watching people walk by. He wished his daughter could be with him now.

He checked his phone for the Mastermind's message, opening it to read the contents: "Departure from Montparnasse for the South of France in two days."

Perfect! He intended to do exactly what the Mastermind had suggested: enjoy Paris for the next two days. He would have plenty of time to relax and enjoy the museums, stores and restaurants. In fact, he already had plans to visit the best vegetarian eateries of the city: Le Potager du Marais, near Les Halles; Au Grains de Folie, in Montmartre; and, saving the best for last, Au Petit Jardin, near the Eiffel Tower.

Life was not too bad after all.

Chapter 45

It was a long flight from Chicago to Paris. We landed in Charles de Gaulle Airport at 5:30 a.m. I was grateful for the toothbrush and shaving kit the FBI agents had provided, and I put them to good use during the course of the flight, while most of the other passengers were asleep in their seats.

I looked out the window to see clear skies, confirming the pilot's announcement that it was to be sunny in Paris, 72 degrees Fahrenheit for the daytime high, and no rain in the forecast.

After waiting for my fellow travelers to get out of their seats, I finally made it out.

Michel was waiting for me at the exit of the plane.

"Salut, cousin!" he said.

"Salut, cousin!" I repeated.

We smiled, shook hands, and then kissed each other on both cheeks.

It was wonderful to speak French again. Even with all the years I'd spent living in the states, French would always be my native language.

"I'll do my best to put up with your American accent, Seb, but you'll have to speak French while you're here," Michel said, laughing.

"No problem," I told him. "It will be a treat for me."

"Great! Come with me. We will get out faster going through the back door. Any luggage?"

"No, just this," I said, indicating the black gym bag. "No time for anything else."

Michel nodded, leading the way.

"I would love an espresso and a chocolate croissant," I said in a pleading tone. "I have a change of clothes in this bag, and I'll go out to get a few things later today."

"No problem," he said. "We will stop for coffee and a croissant on the way to my office. You can change there."

Michel showed his badge to a cop in a cubicle, and I showed the passport the FBI had given me, which was stamped without fanfare, and we were on our way. We exited the terminal and headed toward Michel's vehicle, which was parked in front of the entrance and guarded by a uniformed officer.

"I saved one hour just because I am with Interpol!" Michel said with a grin.

We quickly entered the highway, headed for Paris. Already crowded, the estimated time to reach Porte de la Chapelle was forty-five minutes. Michel put on his flashing light and we passed all the other cars, speeding along the emergency path on the right side of the road. We reached Paris in no time.

"How is the family?" I asked.

"Great! Mom has already started to cook for you. Don't say no because of work; she will hang you. I told her we'll be there at 8:30 tonight."

"Are you kidding? I have been thinking about it ever since I left last night," I replied, my mouth watering. "I never let any case interfere with food!"

We both laughed.

"But for now, we do need to focus on the case," I said. "Any news on our suspect?"

"I have people analyzing the video of the airport right now," Michel said. "We should get something in the middle of the day. Four planes arrived from Chicago yesterday, so it should be pretty easy to spot him."

"He is really good at moving fast," I said. "I hope he will still be in Paris."

"We will find out soon enough, cousin," Michel said. "I will introduce you to the small team I've put in place to help you on this case. The only thing is, you cannot carry a weapon, as you are not technically considered a law enforcement officer here in France."

"I understand."

The Périphérique, the highway that circles Paris, was also jammed, so it took us a little longer to reach the Paris Interpol office.

Michel parked his car in the garage of the building.

"What was it you said about never letting a case interfere with food?" he asked.

I laughed. "I'm glad you brought that up. The frozen pastry and cold coffee on the plane definitely did not satisfy me!"

"A promise is a promise, cousin," Michel said, gesturing toward the café across the street.

So, prior to diving into the case, we stopped to enjoy our breakfast.

Chapter 46

Later in the day, while we were out having lunch, the phone rang in Michel's pocket and he answered it after the second ring.

"Interpol Division, Chief Michel Caravaggio."

I looked at his face as he started to frown and get serious. I could see the same Italian features prominent in many members of my mother's side of the family; I had inherited them as well.

"Thank you, Captain Fourchaud. Please keep me updated. We are on our way," Michel said, putting the phone back in his pocket.

"Seb, our assassin has been spotted in the Latin Quarter. A team has been following him, and he is now having lunch in a restaurant on Avenue de la Bourdonnais. The DGSE has been helping us track him since his arrival in France. They are getting ready to move on him, but they are waiting for us. Let's go now." He stood up, moved away from the table, and motioned for me to follow.

I was impressed. DGSE, Direction Générale de la Sécurité, and part of the Ministry of Defense, was responsible for counter-intelligence in France.

"I will call Mom and tell her we will be late for dinner," Michel added, on a more personal note.

Two minutes later we were crossing Paris in his unmarked car, with sirens blaring through the lunch crowd.

The end of this international chase was near.

Chapter 47

Ever since yesterday, the Handler had felt that something was in the air. Something was bothering him, but he could not pinpoint it. A few times he'd thought he was being followed, and he had changed course and moved around, trying to elude anyone who might be tailing him. He did not see anybody suspicious; still, he did not feel confident.

He sat down at a table in Au Petit Jardin, the new vegetarian eatery he'd been so eager to try. It was in vogue in Paris right now, located just a block east of the Champs de Mars, near the Eiffel Tower. He picked up the menu and looked at the lunch offerings. It was going to be his last meal in the French capital, as the high-speed train to Toulouse was due to leave in a few hours. By tomorrow night everything would be over, and he would be on a plane bound for Washington, DC. He would see his daughter in just two days; he could hardly wait. ...

"Bonjour, monsieur," the waiter said "Our special today is a ratatouille tartine, topped with a fried duck egg and served with a salad. Can I bring you anything to drink? Sparkling water or wine?"

"A glass of crisp Cheverny, please. And I will take the special."

"Excellent, monsieur."

"Where are your restrooms, please?" the Handler asked. "I need to wash my hands."

"On the right side, behind that back door, monsieur." The waiter pointed toward one of the two doors behind him.

The Handler left his napkin on the plate, got up, picked up his backpack and went to the back of the restaurant. He wanted to check for a possible escape route, just in case something happened. He passed the kitchen where he saw two cooks who seemed to be from India or Sri Lanka, plating some fresh salad and grated cheese. Asparagus spears flamed on the grill, next to roasted bell peppers and tomato confit. But what he paid the most attention to was the door behind the two cooks, which provided a potential exit route to the street behind the restaurant.

After washing his hands in the restroom, which had no window, the Handler checked his phone to confirm his train's departure time. It was on time today.

"Good," he said to himself. "No strike today."

He started to relax a little bit, thinking about his return to the states as he returned to his table. The glass of wine was already there, and only three minutes after he sat down, his food arrived.

The dish had an incredible aroma: ratatouille vegetables, fresh oregano and fresh rosemary. A gorgeous deep-yellow duck egg completed the magnificent dish, accompanied by a small salad and a fresh piece of baguette.

"Meersee boocoo," he said in his broken French.

The waiter smiled and then retreated.

The Handler looked at the exquisite array for a moment longer, and then he started to eat.

Just a few minutes later, his phone rang. It was his daughter. "Hi, honey, how are you today? Getting ready to start your day?"

"Yes, Dad. Hey, I can barely hear you ... can you hear me, Dad?"

"Hold on, honey, I'm in a restaurant, and it's very loud. Give me a second. I'll go into the restroom where it's quieter. ..."

Chapter 48

The DGSE reported that the suspect had entered a building that would prove to be the restaurant where he was enjoying his lunch. The police had discreetly blocked access to the avenue and were diverting traffic to adjacent roads.

Michel and I arrived at the scene, pulling up quietly in a dark unmarked sedan. He had turned off the lights and siren a few blocks away. We got out of the car, each of us holding a fuzzy printed image of the suspected killer.

"I am going inside to have a bite to eat, Michel," I told my cousin. "Stay here, and keep your phone on. This restaurant seems to be filled with tourists, and you look like a cop, the way you are dressed and with your buzz cut. Our guy will spot you in a second, and panic. I look like a tourist." I paused and then added, "Is that okay with you?"

"Yes, very good idea, Seb. You will be my eyes inside. Take this radio, and put the small plug in your ear. Please be careful. Remember, I can't let you have a weapon. Just call in, and we will be there in a matter of seconds." Michel gave me a pat on the back and pushed me toward the restaurant.

"Bonjour, monsieur. Bienvenue Au Petit Jardin," said the hostess as I entered the restaurant.

I wanted to appear to be an American tourist, so when she asked how many people were in my party, I answered her in English. "Just one. Could I sit in the back of the restaurant, please?"

"Certainly, sir," she said. "Please follow me."

The smell of fresh basil and rosemary filled the whole restaurant. Parisian gardens were painted all over the inside of the place, and it was busy, even for lunch hour. There had to be at least sixty people inside, speaking in six different languages. Couples and small office groups made up most of the crowd. I was pretty sure our suspect would be alone, but unfortunately, I did not see anyone sitting by himself.

"How is this table, sir?" asked the hostess.

"Perfect," I told her. "Thank you."

I was indeed sitting at the end of the restaurant, with my back to the wall, and had a great view of the dining room. The problem was that I was the only lone diner. The waiter came to me right away, handing me a menu and telling me about the daily special. I ordered a Badoit, said I needed a few moments, and thanked him.

I then pulled my phone out and opened the photo of our suspect. I looked around but did not see anybody who looked like him. I put the phone to my ear and faked a call. Instead, I talked through the radio Michel had given me.

"Michel, I don't see anyone looking like our suspect in here. Are you sure of your information?"

"Affirmative. The DGSE saw him enter the building. Keep looking."

"I will."

I raised my menu in front of me and continued to look at the customers. I then noticed an empty table a few feet away from me, with a half-empty glass of white wine and a half-eaten open face sandwich, which appeared to be topped with a vegetable stew.

"Michel, there is an empty seat by me. No one is at the table. I did not see anybody leave the restaurant. Did you see anybody coming out?"

"Negative. I will send some men in through the back, just in case."

As the waiter came back to take my order, a man passed by me, coming through one of the two back doors. He went directly to the empty table. I caught the last of his conversation before he put his cell phone back in his pocket.

"That's my girl! Glad to hear things are good at school. Hey sweetie, I got to run. See you this week-end", "Love you too."

This was definitely our man. He looked to be about six feet tall, give or take an inch, had a strong physique and very short dark hair threaded with gray. He had an American accent, and was a better-looking man in person than he appeared to be in his photo. He wore a pair of jeans, a black shirt and a lightweight jacket; he carried a backpack. After looking around at all the other tables, including mine, he sat down. He put the backpack on the seat next to him, and I could see an opening in it.

Slowly, he went back to what was left of his lunch and glass of wine.

I could not believe it. The man who had killed my friends was right there in front of me, enjoying his lunch after finishing a pleasant phone call with his daughter, just like any ordinary dad, relaxed and casual. Who was this man? I started to fume but controlled myself very quickly. I was not in my jurisdiction, and my cousin was in charge of the arrest.

"Enjoy your last gourmet meal," I thought. Into the radio I said in a low voice, "Michel, it is a go."

Chapter 49

Everything went very fast after that. I saw Michel enter the restaurant, with two other plainclothes Interpol agents. They were laughing and acting casual, as if they were friends meeting for lunch. The hostess showed them to a table in the middle of the restaurant, and they sat down.

Next, I saw our suspect lift up his head to watch the three men entering the restaurant. He seemed to get nervous for a second, but then as soon as the men sat down, he seemed to relax a bit, and he finished his lunch. I could tell he was keeping an eye on them.

Michel and his agents were doing a great job. At no time did they make eye contact with the suspect.

"Seb," Michel said over the radio, "I have some men in the back alley, in case he makes a run for it. In addition to my Interpol guys, there are some GIGN men hiding behind the kitchen door in back of you. I will head toward the restroom in two minutes, and that's when I'll make the arrest. We need as little agitation as possible in order to avoid casualties. Do not move. Okay?"

"Okay," I responded. GIGN, short for Groupe D'Intervention de la Gendarmerie Nationale, was a special operations unit of the French Armed Forces, responsible for counterterrorism. Together with Interpol and DGSE, I could not ask for better backup. We needed to take the murderer out of here—dead or alive—without harming any innocent people.

I watched Michel get up from the table, making a joke with his agents and then walking toward the restroom. As he walked casually between the tables, headed toward the back of the restaurant, I saw our suspect digging for something in his backpack.

Suddenly, he stood up and raised a .45 in my cousin's direction.

"Gun!" I yelled at the top of my lungs, already up and running in the suspect's direction.

A shot rang out in the restaurant, and I saw a bullet hit Michel in the chest. The suspect then turned around and started to aim at me. Our eyes met for a split second, and I saw no fear in his.

A second shot rang out, and then a red dot appeared on the suspect's forehead. The man fell hard, backwards, leaving a splatter of blood on the white napkins. Traces of what appeared to be brain matter had spattered onto the patrons' vegetarian dishes.

People started to scream, jumping up and running for the exit.

I knew the police were outside and would manage crowd control, so I ran to Michel. He lay on the floor, but no blood seemed to hemorrhage from his body, which was good news.

"Michel … Michel, can you hear me?" I opened his shirt to see a bulletproof vest, with the slug embedded in it. The impact had reduced the slug to half its size. I shuddered when I saw that it was exactly at the level of his heart.

I heard him moan as he slowly regained consciousness, and I squatted beside him, filled with an incredible sense of relief.

"I was not expecting him to shoot point-blank," Michel said. "I did not see that coming."

"You are very lucky, cousin. Very lucky." I called for the paramedics, who were waiting outside, and continued to talk to Michel.

"Don't say anything to my mom," he said. "She will

freak out."

"Quiet," I told him. "You will be fine after you get some painkillers."

He smiled.

"I am still hungry for my favorite dish, which no one can make like my aunt, so you'd better be recovered in time for dinner."

Five minutes later he was lying on a stretcher, and the paramedics wheeled him toward the ambulance.

"I will join you soon, Michel. I want to get more info on our guy," I said as I walked alongside the stretcher. "Do you want me to call Aunt Celina?"

"Yes, but don't say anything about what happened; just tell her we will be a little late."

He waved good-bye, and I responded with a tap on his leg. "You will be fine," I told him.

I heard the ambulance siren echoing between the apartments on the avenue as it traveled to the hospital; I'd heard the paramedics say they were taking Michel to Pitié-Salpêtrière. Outside, all the patrons of the restaurant were segregated from everybody else, and the local police, GIGN, Interpol and the DGSE worked together to process all of them as quickly as possible, trying to get information on the suspect from the witnesses' statements. There was nothing I could do to assist, so I went back inside and returned to the dead body.

The Interpol SWAT team still stood by the back door, talking about what had just happened. I went over to them, introduced myself, and shook the hand of the man who had saved my life a few minutes earlier.

"Great shot! Thank you for saving my life," I said.

"Thank you, sir … you are welcome, sir," he said with a professional smile.

Now I could focus for a few minutes on the mess left by the shooting. The good thing was that nobody else was hurt.

Some of the customers would have bad dreams for a while, but that would pass. The suspect lay on the gray floor with a large pool of blood coming out of the back of his wide-open head. Steam was still coming out of the dishes that customers had left behind during the panic, but there was no smell of food. The odors of sweat and gunpowder overpowered the aromas of basil and tarragon. On a chair by the table of the dead suspect, the backpack was still open. I approached it slowly, and using a knife from one of the serving dishes, I inspected it, hoping to find more evidence, even though I knew we were really close to closing the case.

"Excuse me, sir," I said to the ME who was processing the body. "Can I borrow some latex gloves from you, please?"

"Sure thing," he said. "Here you go."

I took the gloves he handed to me.

Inside the bag were two single folders: a skinny blue and a thick red. Just as I found them, my phone rang.

"Did you find anything interesting, Seb?" Michel asked me.

"Michel, what are you doing? You should rest. We can talk about it later."

"Come on, Seb! We are stuck in a traffic jam, and I have a few minutes to spare," he replied in a lighthearted voice. Obviously, the painkillers administered by the paramedics were having a happy effect on him.

"I don't know yet. I found two folders in his backpack," I replied as I opened the thin one.

To my surprise, I found pictures of a young girl and what seemed to be drawings of horses. The backs of the pictures were all labeled Celeste, and each one had a date noted below the name. They appeared to be photographs of the same girl, taken at different ages.

"Pictures of a young girl," I told Michel. "This must be the daughter he was talking to. There are drawings too, and a note that says 'For Dad, with all my love, wherever you are!' That's it for the skinny folder."

I placed the blue folder on the table, and then I opened the red folder, which was at least two inches thick.

"What else?" Michel asked.

"I'm going through the other folder. Wait a second."

After going through a few pages, I had to sit down. I was stunned by the information I was seeing. In front of me was the whole plan of the killer we had been chasing since the murder of Chef Bob Dewey in Las Vegas. All the notes were handwritten in an American-style notebook. The handwriting itself was beautiful and very classy. Reading slowly, I learned all the research the killer had done on each of his victims. He had spent a whole year planning the events, noting everything, page by page and in chronological order, including the habits and intimate details of all the victims.

I relayed what I read to Michel, and then I flipped to the back to see what the end of the story was. "The last entry talks about a meeting in southwestern France, followed by the letters 'C. D.'"

"Initials probably," said Michel.

"I'll see what I can find out," I told him.

I had an idea what the initials C. D. stood for, but I wanted that to be determined through Interpol's investigation and procedures. We couldn't make the case based on my gut instincts.

Chapter 50

I decided to take the Métro to the hospital to pick up Michel. It was now 5:00 p.m., and the traffic in Paris was heavy. I walked through the Champs de Mars, admiring the beautiful Tour Eiffel as I headed toward L'École Militaire, turning right on Place Joffre to reach the elevated station of La Motte-Picquet. I purchased a single pass and took the number 6 line, a straight shot to Chevaleret, which was located at the entrance to the immense hospital complex. The Métro was packed with people returning home at the end of the workday.

The train reached my stop pretty quickly, and I got out in front of the hospital and headed toward the emergency room. After taking a few wrong turns in this gigantic labyrinth of a building—it was the largest hospital in the world at the time of the French Revolution, with more than ten thousand beds—I finally made it to the second emergency room in the facility. There I found my cousin, putting his shirt back on and talking with a good-looking nurse dressed in a blue outfit. They were laughing about something.

"Sorry to interrupt," I said as I knocked on the door.

The air was warm inside the room, and the windows were open to allow fresh air to circulate. French hospitals had no air conditioning because of the belief that recycled air could carry airborne diseases.

"No, no, come on in, cousin," Michel said. "I was just talking to Nurse Jacqueline, telling her the story of how, when we were five years old, you made a fool of yourself at the beach in Deauville. Do you remember?"

"As I recall, it seems to be the official family story. Your dad even told that joke at my wedding." I paused as I put my lightweight jacket at the foot of the bed, and then I said, "Jacqueline, don't believe a word this man says. He has the tendency to exaggerate a little."

"I had a feeling," she said, smiling. "Michel, it was still nice to meet you. Remember to take it easy for a few days, as you have two bruised ribs."

She wrote on the paper on her clipboard and then asked him to sign the discharge.

"Thank you, Jacqueline. I will see you soon," Michel said. He then kissed her on both cheeks, as if they were friends.

"Of course," she said. "Good-bye, Michel." As she walked past me on her way to the door, she smiled and said, "Good-bye, Wet Boy."

"Good night, Jacqueline," I replied, looking at my cousin, who seemed to be suffering from nothing but laughing too much.

"It hurts my ribs to laugh like that!" he said, confirming my deduction.

I rolled my eyes at him. "Are you ready, idiot?" I asked, adding, "I am hungry for my aunt's food, so put on your shoes, and let's move. We still have to get your car at your office."

"There is a patrol car waiting to take us back there now. I already called them. We will talk about the case en route."

We went down the stairs, exited the building and walked a good five minutes to meet the car waiting for us on Boulevard de l'Hôpital, located on the north side of the hospital, near the Austerlitz station.

From there, we took Les Quais, bordering the Seine. The patrol car sped along, siren blaring, as we headed north to the Interpol office.

"Let me see the file, please," Michel said.

"A lot of details," I said, giving him the file. "Three planned murders in one week! The pace of his actions has left me speechless." The fourth victim, Master Chef LeJeune's friend, had been accounted for in the plan because the murderer knew the man would be at the cabin, fishing with the chef.

As we went over the contents of the red file folder we passed Île Saint-Louis on our right, and then Île de a Cité, with Notre-Dame Cathedral.

"We need to find out what the letters 'C. D.' stands for," Michel said.

"I agree," I replied. "I believe they could be the initials of the mastermind of this case. The suspect came to Paris not only to finish his work but also to be paid, I think."

"Could be," Michel said. "Let's check the info we have in this folder, and then I'll have my people check it against our Interpol info. We'll see if something comes up."

"Sounds good," I said.

Siren still blaring, we zipped through the heavy traffic, and I caught a glimpse of the beautiful Musée d'Orsay. Our driver was obviously used to driving in Paris during rush hour! Just a few seconds later, we turned right on Pont Alexandre III, the magnificent arch bridge in front of the majestic Hôtel des Invalides, created by Napoleon Bonaparte. We then drove along Avenue Winston Churchill, past the Grand Palais, whose beautiful glass roof made the building an amazing exhibition hall.

"This town is gorgeous!" I said.

"It is," Michel responded. "But when you live in it, you know, unfortunately, you do not enjoy it as much."

With that, we crossed the Champs-Élysées. We were now only a few minutes from the Interpol office.

Chapter 51

After spending a good hour on Highway A13, headed for my aunt and uncle's house, we arrived at our destination at around 8:30 p.m. We entered the beautiful countryside property, west of Paris and the banlieues (suburbs). Pauli, my uncle's German shepherd, greeted us. The dog barked at us at first but calmed down when he recognized Michel. He then came and sniffed me, determined after a few seconds that I was not dangerous, and then went back toward the garden.

"Bastiano!" my uncle Giovanni Caravaggio said from the front steps of the house. "How are you doing, my nephew?"

We kissed as Latin families do, and he pulled me inside to greet my aunt, who was working the pots in the kitchen.

My nostrils doubled in size as I entered the cooking sanctuary. The mixed aroma of spices, garlic, onion, pepper and frying oil filled the room. I recognized that smell. In honor of my visit, my aunt Celina was preparing my favorite dish—the one I had been dreaming about all day.

Seeing me, she wiped her hands on her apron and then gave me a huge hug. "So happy you could come and have dinner with us," she said, beaming her Creole smile.

"I have been waiting for this meal ever since I landed in Paris," I told her as I slowly walked to the stove to take a peek at what would be in my belly in a few minutes.

Pop! Uncle Giovanni opened a bottle of champagne and started pouring it into flutes.

"Come outside to see my garden," he said, handing Michel and me each a glass.

Going through the open French doors in the kitchen, we

stepped out onto the patio where a beautiful, crystal-clear blue pool greeted us. We went past it, sipping our champagne, and walked on to his garden. The weather was very pleasant; crickets sang in the background, and the smell of fresh herbs got stronger and stronger as we approached the work of art.

In front of us was a perfect layered garden. One side housed all the fresh herbs, such as basil, thyme, rosemary and sage. Onion, garlic and lettuce were planted in perfect rows, all at perfect maturity. Zucchini and eggplant lay on the ground, ready to be picked. Red tomatoes on the vine dangled from the trellis, luscious and inviting.

Uncle Giovanni proudly picked two tomatoes, one for Michel and one for me, and we bit into them hungrily. A rush of soft flesh and sweetness burst in my mouth. I recognized right away where those tomatoes came from. Many years ago, my mom had given my uncle seeds from Mount Vesuvius, the volcano near Naples, Italy. She and my dad had traveled there on vacation. Uncle Giovanni had kept the seeds, planting tomatoes every year since.

"What do you think?" my uncle asked me.

"Impressive, I have to admit," I said, swallowing. "That's a lot of produce," I added, gesturing toward the entire garden. "Do you use them all?"

"We can for the winter, and we give a lot to your cousin. The Interpol office loves the treats!" he replied with a wink.

I finished my champagne, smiling at my uncle. Every ingredient in tonight's main dish had come from this garden. I loved that. Even the chickens were raised on the premises.

When I closed my eyes, the smell of all those herbs transported me to the South of France, where garrigue and lavender were king and queen.

"Come inside!" my aunt yelled from the kitchen. "Dinner is ready."

I was so happy to be there. Visiting my aunt and uncle was a must-do pilgrimage whenever I went to France. Those few hours sustained me for a whole year.

"Go down to the cellar and get some wine, Bastiano," Uncle Giovanni said. "Michel, go with him. Take whatever you want."

A pilgrimage within a pilgrimage: the visit to my uncle's wine cave.

I called most of his reserve "mystery bottles," as the natural humidity removed the labels from certain bottles. I could recognize bottles by shape, but the year was a little more difficult to determine. All the wines with partial labels were often more than ten years old. I started with a 2011 Reserve Cabernet Franc from the Loire valley, then took a 2005 Châteauneuf-du-Pape, and to finish the meal, one of the mystery bottles, an aged Bordeaux.

For appetizers, we had fried cod accra, served with a spicy homemade mayonnaise and spicy blood sausage. Chicken stewed in turmeric, onion, tomato and garlic, served with sticky white rice and green lentils was the main entrée. After that, we had a cheese tray and salad. Dessert was a thick chocolate mousse.

Dinner went on for three hours. As we savored the delicious meal we talked about everything: family, politics, friends, business and food. After drinking three bottles of wine, plus the flutes of champagne, we did not feel drunk at all, as we were eating and drinking at the same time. Michel and I also planned to spend the night, so we did not need to be concerned about driving back to Paris. Staying overnight at my aunt and uncle's was another memorable souvenir for me.

For me, the optimum pairing was the chocolate mousse and the Bordeaux. I had asked my aunt for the recipe for the mousse so we could add it to the menu at the Drunken Frog. We did try it in Omaha, but for whatever reason, we could never completely replicate it. Perhaps no one could make that mousse quite as well as she did.

By 1:00 a.m., after helping my aunt clean up the table and kitchen, we were headed for our rooms.

My stomach was full, my head was light, and I did feel a tiny bit drunk. But I was also very happy. After two deep breaths I fell asleep and dreamed of Vesuvius, Pompeii and Naples.

Chapter 52

"Wake up, Seb! Time to go!"

I heard the words on the periphery of wakefulness. I was still walking alongside the Italian volcano. "Earthquake!" I said, still half-asleep.

"No, it's just me."

Opening my eyes, I saw Michel standing over me.

He grinned. "It's 6:00 a.m., cousin. Coffee is ready. I just got a call from the office: they found out who 'C. D.' is."

After a quick shower I said my good-byes to my generous hosts, telling them I hoped to see them soon. I promised I would bring Tom with me the next time I came to France.

By 6:30 a.m. we were on the road, headed back to Paris. We had the police light on, so even with the morning traffic jam, it took us only twenty-five minutes to get to the office.

At 7:00 a.m. we were in a briefing room with all the agents on the case.

Captain Fourchaud entered the room holding an iPad. After a quick hello, he explained what they had discovered during the night.

"Charles Dumont, ex-entrepreneur, made millions in the agro industry," he said. "He sold his company to a multinational group from Switzerland almost ten years ago. He's divorced, currently single. His ex-wife, Jocelyn, is remarried. Her current husband is a famous antique dealer in the city of Bordeaux. It appears that the exes have not kept in touch over the years. They had a daughter who died when she was ten. Dumont lives alone in southwestern France. No known prior arrests; good citizen; no trouble."

Michel said, "That does not make him an accessory to murder."

"No, it doesn't," said the captain. "But we've been looking into him ever since you asked us to check him out."

"Yes," I said. "Charles Dumont is the man I asked you to look into, Michel, based on information from the attorney handling the massive Las Vegas lawsuit involving the murdered chefs." I shook my head in disbelief. "I still don't understand why a law-abiding citizen would become involved in murder."

"I'm getting to that," said the captain, looking directly at me. "The attorney you spoke to was correct: Dumont's daughter died as a result of the E. coli outbreak in Las Vegas."

"If that's true, I can't blame the guy, really," said Michel. "I would be going crazy as well. Probably pissed off at the whole world too."

"True, but I believe there are better ways to seek justice. Killing people is not the answer," I said.

"Do you have the address of Charles Dumont, Captain?" Michel asked.

"Yes, Chief. I already contacted a gendarmerie in the south. The private jet is scheduled to depart in one hour, taking you from Paris-Le Bourget Airport straight to Tarbes. You can arrest Dumont at his estate."

Chapter 53

Charles Dumont stood on his cozy terrace and looked out at his large estate, a faded smile on his face. It was 6:35 a.m., and a thin white fog was floating over the hills, veiling them in pale mist. A large green pasture extended from the right of the property, and he could see some of his livestock grazing on the fresh grass. Lambs, sheep and a few Charolais cows ambled peacefully. On the left, rows of vineyards lined the wall surrounding the property. He could see fruit hanging, and he knew it was only a matter of days before the harvest of his organic grapes was due. The morning temperature was the most comfortable of the day, as the heat was still persistent during these last days of summer

He finished his second espresso of the day. With tears in his eyes, he entered his 150-year-old kitchen, remodeled with the most-advanced appliances. He loved the mix of the old building and the modern conveniences. He remembered buying this estate twenty years ago, when it was a large old farm with numerous dilapidated dependencies. He'd toured the property with his then wife, Jocelyn, and they'd both fallen in love with the region and the domain. A lot of work had to be done to rebuild the house, plant the vineyard and start an organic farm; but, it had been worth all the effort, just as he'd known it would be. He had achieved his dream.

Charles Dumont had wanted to live here with his family, far away from the craziness of the industrial world and the big cities, where he was getting lost. He remembered making the best decision of his life in 2000, when he sold his company in Paris. A multinational company based in Switzerland had paid a few hundred million US dollars for his products and patents. Shortly after the eighth birthday of his daughter, Emilia, the whole family had finally moved to southwestern France, to the estate that had been their summer house. The vineyard, already in its third year of production, had experienced enormous success, getting great reviews from Le Point *magazine,* Le Guide Hachette *and even Robert Parker in the US.*

Only forty-six years old at that time, Charles Dumont had proved to himself and his family that he was on the top of the world. Nothing could shatter his great life.

At the thought, he went to his espresso machine and made himself a third coffee. The aroma of the freshly roasted beans filled the room, and the smell of the freshly baked croissant on the table made his stomach growl. Even if he did not feel hungry, he knew he had to eat something. The stress of the past few weeks was getting to him, and he was anxious for it all to end, to finally be over. A few more days, and everything would be better. He sat down at the massive wooden table in the kitchen, alone with his coffee and croissant, and looked at the beautiful picture of his family: Jocelyn, Emilia and him, together in Quebec, Canada, more than ten years ago.

What a fun vacation that was. They'd left Charles de Gaulle Airport a few days after the end of his daughter's school year, flying to New York City for a tour of the US East Coast and the region of Quebec in Canada, and finishing up on the West Coast of the US. He'd had the chance to travel to Chicago and Washington, DC a few times, and his wife was excited to go back to the Big Apple, as she'd been an exchange student there when she was a teenager. She had stayed with a host family on the Jersey Shore and had traveled to the big city to see Broadway shows and take in the sights: Chinatown, Little Italy, the New York Stock Exchange, the Empire State Building, the Statue of Liberty and many other famous landmarks. She wanted her husband and daughter to see what she had enjoyed when she was young. And it was amazing. Even though New York was not the safest tourist spot at that time, the grandiosity of the city, with its skyscrapers, yellow cabs and hot-dog stands on every corner, was fantastic to experience. Everything in the American movies was there! He smiled now, remembering Emilia with her big eyes wide open, just thirsty for the learning experience, absorbing the images and eager to engage in conversation. All the Americans they met found her adorable, especially her French accent.

Charles Dumont sat back in his chair and looked around his kitchen. His head ached. He had not slept well the last two nights. He was tired, especially of being alone. He missed his family so much. Tears started to come to his eyes as he focused on a child's drawing on the fridge. In their hotel room in Las Vegas Emilia had drawn a summary of their US trip: the Empire State Building, Mickey Mouse at Disneyland, the Hollywood sign and a princess in front of a white castle with red and blue towers. These were her favorite memories of the trip. The happy moments of the trip abruptly ended with his recollection of the painful experience in Las Vegas.

He sipped his coffee, turned his thoughts to the present time, picked up his cell phone, scrolled to the familiar number and pressed Call. The Handler did not answer the phone, which meant something had gone wrong.

Nausea overcame Charles Dumont at that moment, and he started to vomit all over the floor of his luxurious kitchen.

Chapter 54

We boarded the Falcon 300 at 8:00 a.m., flying toward the city of Pau. No need to take our shoes off, screen our bags and get X-rayed this time; we took off immediately, and the flight aboard the private jet would not last more than about an hour. The gendarmerie (police) from the Tarbes precinct would be waiting on the ground to drive us to Madiran, the small but famous wine community where our suspected criminal mastermind lived.

"This Charles Dumont spent years planning this murder," I said to my cousin as we traveled thirty-five thousand feet above the beautiful countryside of France.

"How would you feel if you lost Tom because of a food-borne illness?" Michel asked softly.

"I would be pissed off, because most food-borne illness can be prevented," I replied, more as a restaurant owner than a cop.

"Exactly my point" Michel said, adding, "Ultimately the bosses are the ones responsible, and they are the ones who need to be held accountable for the mistakes."

"I understand that, but those chefs were my friends. Besides, there are a lot more people who are responsible for food safety other than chefs and restaurateurs," I said. "For example, there is the USDA in the United States, which is supposed to be in charge of food safety for the entire country, but the reality is that this department is overwhelmed, understaffed and pressured by lobbyists, big money, and politicians in Washington, DC. Food and food production are such an important part of the economy that the industry's power very often trumps the safety of the products, the workers and ultimately, the consumers. The stores and restaurants selling the food to customers can only do so much to ensure food safety."

Michel looked at me. "You are talking like a chef, not a detective, cousin, but I hear what you're saying," he said. "It is pretty much the same here in France. Our economy relies on agriculture and food production, and we are proud of our products; still, there are abuses at every level. Remember the scandal a few years back, when ground meat was found to contain horse meat coming from Romania?"

"Yes. I remember you telling me about it, and it made news in the US as well. Scandals like that actually help strengthen the safety of the chains of production. Here in France it is now mandatory to trace where the product is from, as well as its path to the market. We are getting there in the US, but once again, things are moving very slowly. There is a return to the farmers' market concept: the person who produces the goods sells directly to the end consumer. In the US, we call it 'farm to table.'"

"Like in our grandmother's day!"

"Exactly."

"It's sad what has happened to food," Michel said. "Even when I visited the French island of Guadeloupe in the Caribbean, the bananas were cut while still green and shipped to the home country, turning yellow during the journey. Same thing with tomatoes from Holland; there is no sun there, so everything is produced in greenhouses. They ship the tomatoes green and put them in special transport trucks that help them ripen in route, so when they arrive in stores or restaurants, they're red. The result is that you can get every food product all year long, but it will have absolutely no flavor."

"That's right," I agreed. "It's also why your father's tomatoes tasted so wonderful last night! And everything else from the garden too. There's nothing better than homemade, home-grown food." I smiled, remembering the delicious tastes and aromas of our dinner the night before. Then, with my smile fading, I added, "With worldwide overpopulation, it's clear that food production will continue to be a serious ongoing problem. What annoys me the most is the power of those multinational companies that dictate what everybody eats, and what everybody has to pay in order to eat."

"I agree with you on all that," Michel said.

I paused for a second and then said, "Well, this discussion can go on for a long time, cousin. All I can say is, I am so glad to see small-scale producers and farmers' markets gaining ground all over the world. It is turning things around; people are fed up with being fed crap."

Michel laughed.

"Your mom's food was outstanding last night, as was your dad's wine," I said, even though I'd already told this to my aunt, uncle and cousin many times.

"Thank you again," he said. "They like to host people who appreciate food and wine, especially you, cousin! After all, you are the restaurateur of the family, and we're all so proud of your success."

"Thanks, cousin," I replied, and then I turned to look out the window as I felt our final descent begin.

After the plane touched down and taxied toward the private hangars at the end of the airport, I spotted a Peugeot waiting for us on the tarmac. As the plane's doors opened, a whiff of fuel got into my nostrils, and I was glad to step out into the fresh air. It was still early, but I could already feel the promise of a hot day in the abundant sunshine.

"I'm Lieutenant Pierre Desjardins," said a tall dark-haired man dressed in civilian clothes. Greeting us with a firm handshake, he added, "This is Sergeant Alexis Salles, my second in command; he will be driving the car."

Michel and I introduced ourselves, and all four of us got into the car.

As Sergeant Salles started the engine, Lieutenant Desjardins said from the front passenger seat, "We have a forty minute drive to the town of Madiran. I already sent my RAID team ahead; they are waiting for us at the gendarmerie."

"RAID stands for Recherche, Assistance, Intervention and Dissuasion," Michel told me. "Pretty much your local SWAT team."

Sergeant Salles pulled out of the airfield and we sped away, lights flashing and siren blaring, to what I hoped was going to be a simple arrest.

Chapter 55

After cleaning up the kitchen, Charles Dumont went down to his cellar. Entering a vast room with beautiful wood logs on the ceiling and walls of solid rock, he headed toward a vault. There was an electronic keypad on the right side of the door. He punched in a five-digit code, and the sound of the vault's opening system resonated in the empty chamber.

Inside was an impressive wine cellar with more than three thousand bottles maintained at a constant natural temperature of 60 degrees Fahrenheit. A wine lover, he had collected the bottles for many years, hoping to share every vintage with his family. Labels on the bottles indicated the country of origin for each wine, as well as every sub region. He stopped in front of the Burgundy region, looking around for a few moments before taking out a bottle. Moving toward the high table in the middle of the room, he set down the bottle and picked out a Spiegelau Pinot Noir wineglass. He opened the bottle, poured some of the precious liquid into the glass and let it sit for a moment. Sitting on a wrought-iron chair he reached for the glass, bringing it to his nose and smelling it, and then he swirled it around and set it back on the table.

"A few more minutes," he murmured.

He stood up and walked to another door, located between the Napa Valley and Australian wines, where another keypad was located. He punched in a different code and opened that door as well. This room held a few handguns, some other types of weaponry and boxes of ammunition. Video screens on one wall showed live views of the gate entrance, the driveway, the outside of the house, the various barns and the winery. After checking each screen for any movement, he picked up his favorite hunting shotgun and loaded it with two bullets.

He went back to his wine, put the shotgun on the table, sat in the chair and sipped slowly. "Oh yes," he whispered. "There is nothing to compare to this." He took another sip, took his phone out of his pocket and dialed a number.

After a few rings a familiar female voice answered the phone. "Lafont Antique Shop. How may I help you?"

He knew it was his ex-wife on the other end of the line, but he said, "Jocelyn Lafont, please."

"Speaking."

"Hi, Jocelyn. It's Charles. How are you?"

"Charles?" She sounded surprised. "Is everything all right?"

"Yes. I just wanted to hear your voice. I am not having a good day, and I thought you could talk to me a little bit."

"I don't have time now, Charles. We have customers."

"I understand, but … it's just that it is Emilia's birthday tomorrow and I needed someone to share my pain."

"I am still in pain too, Charles, and I know very well Emilia would have turned twenty-three tomorrow if she had lived, but she didn't. She's gone and we cannot live in the past. You have to move on. I still love her, and I will never forget her, but I cannot bring her back, and neither can you. You really must get on with your life, Charles."

"I did something bad, Jocelyn," Charles said in a soft voice.

Jocelyn was silent on the other end of the line.

After a few seconds, he said, "I took care of what you asked me to."

"What are you talking about?"

"After Emilia's death you asked me to punish the people responsible. Remember? Well, I did it."

"What did you do, Charles?" Jocelyn asked.

He could hear the concern in her soft tone. "I could not stand it any longer," he said. "Knowing they were alive and well, but Emilia was gone. I could no longer endure it. They destroyed our lives, and they had to pay for the crime they committed."

"Oh my God!" Jocelyn said. "Charles, please tell me what you did."

"I took care of those arrogant chefs who poisoned our daughter! I took what they took from her—from us!" he shouted into the phone. "I did what you asked."

"You did what?" Jocelyn exclaimed. "I never told you to kill anybody! I may have said something in the heat of the moment as I was grieving for our daughter, but you can't put this on me. I never asked you to do such a monstrous thing."

"I did it for the whole family," he said.

Charles Dumont started to cry. He took a sip of wine and listened to the silence on the other end of the line.

"Did you do it personally?" Jocelyn finally asked in a calmer tone.

"No. I hired someone. I have not heard from him for two days now, and we were supposed to meet in Toulouse tomorrow so that I could pay him. I believe he has been caught."

"You need to go to the police, Charles," Jocelyn said. "You need to confess and surrender right now. You cannot continue with this existence."

"I am so sorry, Jocelyn, but I did it for us and for our little Emilia."

"Charles, losing Emilia changed you. You have not been the same since her death. Please do something for yourself and for Emilia. Please give yourself up! You cannot go on living like this."

"I have to go, Jocelyn. I will talk to you soon."

He ended the call abruptly and put down the phone.

He sat in the chair, still crying, and the tears tasted salty as they streamed down his face and into his mouth. After a few *minutes he calmed down and stopped crying. His breathing had returned to normal by the time he heard a noise outside the wine cellar. It sounded like a helicopter.*

Chapter 56

We arrived at the Madiran gendarmerie thirty minutes after leaving the tarmac. Sergeant Salles had the siren blaring all the way, but even so, it was obvious he was an excellent driver. He told us he raced cars at the local level, and he surely showed off his skills that day.

As we drove Lieutenant Desjardins was on the radio with the RAID team, getting maps ready and gaining intel on the property we were going to search. It was a vast compound, with one road to the main house, and it had a total of four other buildings, including two barns, storage space for agricultural equipment and machinery and a large winery. The plan was to split into five teams and raid all the buildings on the property at the same time.

"Here we are," Sergeant Salles said as he parked the car in front of a beautiful stone house just outside the village.

We got out and Lieutenant Desjardins introduced Michel and me to the rest of his team, a total of twenty men, all dressed in dark camouflage gear.

The squad leader, Sergeant Panton, provided a quick synopsis of the situation. "Here are some maps of the village," he said, handing us each a printout. "We are located here, to the south of town, and the property is on the north side. We will have to cross the center of the village, but we will just look like an odd convoy. I'm not worried about that." He smiled, adding, "This map is a satellite image of the suspect's compound, compliments of the DGSE in Paris. It was taken two hours ago. No sign of movement except for the animals."

Sergeant Panton held up the image for all of us to see.

Lieutenant Desjardins took over. "Good work, Sergeant. Thank you. We will split into five teams now, as I discussed with everyone earlier: red, blue, green, black and white. Each team will be responsible for searching and securing one of the buildings on the property. The red team will have more men, so that team will be responsible for the main house."

The tension mounted with each minute that passed. We were all very focused, and each one of us knew what to do.

Michel and I were assigned to the red team, and the lieutenant gave me a Taser, instead of an SP2022, the official handgun of the French gendarmerie. Michel was still responsible for me; I was not a police officer in France. I put on the RAID bulletproof vest the lieutenant gave me and followed my cousin.

Some team members carried FAMAS F1s, very handy weapons capable of delivering traumatic results. Others had weapons that fired rubber bullets, and a few carried tear-gas guns.

Pumped up on adrenaline, and with our earpieces live, we all headed toward our respective vehicles and took off to make the arrest. It was going to be an intense few minutes driving across Madiran.

Lieutenant Desjardins had changed clothes and was now suited up like his men. With masks and helmets in hand, we took off in the Peugeot, this time without the siren.

Sergeant Salles drove, and two unmarked gendarmerie vans followed us.

Nobody in the street paid much attention to us. An older gentleman carrying his morning baguette and newspaper did see us, and signaled us to pass, looking troubled at the sight of something out of the ordinary during his daily walk in the small village.

During our short drive it was hard not to notice the beautiful vineyards around us. This region produced an amazing red, made with the Tannat grape, and I was happy when I found some to put on the wine list at the Drunken Frog. Very harsh when young, the bottles needed years of cellaring for the tannins to mellow. But patience would pay off, as this wine was exceptional, especially with red meat and the duck specialties of this region.

"This is the end of your chase, Seb," Michel said, interrupting my reverie and pushing me out of chef mode.

This was just as well. I needed to be 100 percent detective for the task ahead. "Yes, it is, cousin," I said. Hopefully, everything will go fine. We don't really know the man we're about to arrest. He planned the murders, but he did not pull the trigger."

"He didn't have to," Michel said. "He had enough money to pay a professional hit man to do it. We read the notes, Seb. The treatment of each of the bodies was ordered by this guy."

"I know," I said. "I keep wondering why he was that set on such gruesome revenge."

"He was desperate," Michel said. "Wouldn't you be if it were Tom? I know I would be if it were my family."

I didn't have a chance to answer, as the convoy stopped. We were just a few hundred yards from the entrance to the property.

It wouldn't be long now.

Chapter 57

"There are cameras by the entrance gate," Sergeant Panton said. "Each team knows which building to enter."

Lieutenant Desjardins said, "I will lead the red team; Sergeant Salles will lead the black team; Sergeant Panton will lead the green team; Sergeant Defour will lead the white team; Corporal Étienne will lead the blue team."

We all acknowledged our placement on the respective teams.

"Any questions, gentlemen?" asked Lieutenant Desjardins. When we all shook our heads no, he added, "Everything should be over in less than ten minutes. Thank you, stay safe and keep all communication lines open."

With that said, all the teams started to run toward their respective destinations. We hoped for the advantage of surprise, but experience had long since proved that no one was ever completely prepared to confront a desperate man.

In less than two minutes we were only thirty feet from the main house, hiding behind some bushes.

The house was a pure country French beauty, designed to always be open to the air in the moderate climate. The shutters on many of the windows were closed. That in itself was not a good sign.

I did not have the luxury of enjoying the view. Seconds later, Lieutenant Desjardins' voice over the radio brought me back to reality. "Team red in position."

Each of the other team leaders reported that their teams were also in position.

After what seemed like hours, but was only a few

seconds later, the lieutenant shouted, "It's go time! *Go! Go! Go!*"

Simultaneously, I could hear and envision all the men on the other teams entering each building on the property. I could hear breaking glass and yelling from behind the house as two men from the red team entered by the French doors at the back of the terrace. Two others entered by the kitchen door, and the rest of us broke through the glass window of a large bedroom located on the main floor.

In a matter of minutes the main floor was secured, and men were starting to go up the stairs to check the second floor.

"This is the white team. The barn is secured; nobody on the premises. Over."

"Heard," said the lieutenant. "Leave two men there. The rest of you, join us at the main house."

"Yes, sir."

"This is the green team. The winery is secured. We are advancing to the barrel room."

"Roger that!" said Lieutenant Desjardins.

"This is the blue team. The horse barn is secured."

"Leave two men there, and come to the main house."

"Yes, sir."

"This is the black team. The equipment unit is secure. Nothing but tractors and mowers."

"All right," said the lieutenant. "Leave two men there, and head over to the house."

Everything seemed to be going okay so far. The suspect had to be in the house or outside on the property.

"Two cars in the garage," one of the men said in a low voice.

Two minutes later the red team members upstairs told us via the radio that the second floor was empty.

We all met in the huge living room decorated magnificently in country French style.

"Check for basement doors," Lieutenant Desjardins said.

Old French houses usually didn't have basements, but this was no ordinary property. The owner had clearly spent a lot of money on this estate, so it would not be a surprise if he had built a below-ground level.

While the men sent by the lieutenant went to look for access to a subterranean area, I started to walk around the house, stopping in front of what seemed to be a small bedroom. The door was ajar and I slowly pushed it open, immediately saddened as I walked inside.

All the walls were painted pink and covered with Disney characters. There was a small bed against one wall near a window. The dolls, books, mirror and play makeup set all were definite signs that a young girl occupied the room. Or *had* once occupied it.

There were framed photos everywhere, and one of them caught my eye. It was a picture of a couple, with a young girl between them, standing in front of Above the Stars in Las Vegas. I felt my heart leap into my throat.

"I found a door," I heard someone say over the radio. "It's in the library, hidden behind a bookcase."

I left the girl's bedroom and headed to the opposite side of the house, where the library was located.

After inspecting the door behind the bookcase, Lieutenant Desjardins decided to open the door. It did not look booby-trapped. Painted concrete stairs led downward, turning to the right, with adequate lighting throughout.

"Take a look," the lieutenant said to Sergeant Panton.

"Yes, sir."

Slowly descending the stairs, gun drawn, Sergeant Panton reached the bottom. "Clear!" he said over the radio. "Sir, it appears to be an office. There's a computer, and one wall has maps on it."

"We're coming down, Sergeant," the lieutenant said.

The rest of us joined Sergeant Panton a few seconds later, and we started to inspect the room that clearly was an office.

Our man still was nowhere in sight, and I was starting to feel extremely frustrated.

"Check this out, cousin," Michel said, pointing to a US map on the wall. "Las Vegas, Omaha and Chicago are all circled in red, with dates from last week."

"So I see," I said. "That's the work of our mastermind, for sure."

"Lieutenant," one of the men said. "I found a keypad beside what seems to be another door."

Chapter 58

Thanks to the video surveillance, Charles Dumont knew that the time had arrived. There were twenty-odd men on the property, all heavily armed and determined to get him. He watched them onscreen. At that very moment, they were right on the other side of the heavy wooden door.

He took another sip of his wine.

"It is getting better every second," he murmured. "Spices and floral notes on the nose; medium weight. Very yummy."

He looked at the photo of his daughter in the beautifully carved wooden frame. "I so wished we could have drunk this one together, honey," he said.

The bottle was now half empty, and the comforting warmth of the wine in the chilly cellar had lifted his spirits just a bit. He closed his eyes and started to drift off, content with the memories of his wife and daughter during happy times. He'd had everything going for him at one time: a successful career, a wonderful marriage and a beautiful child who had made his life complete. All that only lasted until the final day of Emilia's lifetime. He remembered the details of that horrible day as if it all had happened only yesterday.

It was the early hours of the morning. They were at the emergency room of the hospital in Pau, the city closest to their home, having driven there during the previous night. After a few days of what originally seemed to be a bad cold, Emilia's condition had worsened rapidly. Two visits to the local physician had brought no improvement, so he and Jocelyn decided to take Emilia to the hospital ER in Pau.

After a few hours of agony and a long wait through the middle of the night, a doctor approached them. His head was down, and he walked toward them slowly, seeming to bear the weight of a thousand pounds on his shoulders.

Jocelyn knew right away. She stood up, screaming, "Oh no! No-o-o-o!"

Charles stood up too, just in time to catch his wife as she passed out. He held Jocelyn in his arms, and his eyes instantly filled with tears.

"I am sorry to tell you that Emilia passed away," the doctor said in a soft, sad tone. "I am so sorry, but there was nothing we could do—nothing that could have been done anywhere. It was too late."

"What exactly happened, Doc?" Charles asked, still holding Jocelyn, as the doctor tried to revive her.

"Poison or a bad bacteria," the doctor said. "Emilia's whole system crashed. Her kidneys failed. She had this in her for a few days before it activated. Have you traveled to a foreign country recently?"

"We just came back from vacation in the United States," Charles answered, dumbfounded by the question. "We were not in Africa or Asia."

"We will do a full autopsy, if you allow us to. I believe that will enable us to narrow down the exact cause of death."

"Yes, absolutely," Charles said. "I want to know exactly what happened, and as soon as possible."

The doctor nodded, easing Jocelyn into a chair. She was conscious, but pale and disoriented. "Nurse!" he called out. "Please help Mrs. Dumont."

Turning back to Charles, the doctor said, "We will let you and your wife know all the information as soon as we have it, Mr. Dumont. Again, I am so very sorry."

With that, he turned around, obviously lighter now that the bad news was given. His white coat disappeared at the end *of the green-painted wall of the ER.*

Charles waited until the nurse said he could take Jocelyn home, but it was the beginning of the end of everything beautiful and happy in his life. At the moment of Emilia's death, his life turned upside down, and his dream of the perfect family was shattered by the actions of a reckless person and system. After the final cause of death was attributed to a rare acute case of E. coli from some unsafe food in Las Vegas, he knew what he had to do. His grief turned to rage, and he wanted revenge.

"Charles Dumont!" he heard a voice calling from the other side of the door. "Are you in there?" the same voice asked again, a few seconds later.

This roused Charles Dumont out of his reverie, and he stood up with his shotgun in his right hand.

Chapter 59

"This is Interpol Division Chief Michel Caravaggio! We have a warrant for your arrest on three counts of conspiracy to commit murder in the United States. Please come out with your hands on your head!"

After a few minutes of silence, Charles Dumont finally answered. "I am almost done with my wine. Please give me a few more minutes."

"Sir, we will have to break down the door if you do not surrender right now," my cousin said.

At that point, I took Michel's arm. "Let me have a minute with him, try to reason with him."

Having found his arsenal, we knew he had a shotgun with him. He had nothing left to live for, so I wanted to go easy, try to talk him into surrendering, so we wouldn't have to go through a shoot-out.

"You have three minutes, Seb," Michel told me.

"Thank you, cousin," I said as I walked toward the door.

"Mr. Dumont," I said slowly, "my name in Sebastien Saint-Gemmes, and I am a detective in Omaha, Nebraska, in the United States. I have been tracking the murderer ever since he killed Chef Bob Dewey in Las Vegas. I returned to Omaha, where he killed Chef Patsy Williams, and tracked him to Iowa, where he killed Master Chef Pierre LeJeune and another man." I paused, and then added, "But you already know all this, as you were expecting to see the killer tomorrow. Unfortunately for you, he was killed yesterday in Paris, in a shoot-out with the police. That's why you did not hear from him."

I waited a few seconds to see if Charles Dumont was

going to say anything, but he didn't, so I continued. "Those chefs you ordered to be killed were my friends, and they never hurt anyone. I am so sorry for the loss of your child, but I believe there were better ways to get justice than to seek revenge by killing people with families."

"What do you know about family, Detective?" Charles Dumont asked through the thick door. "Do you even have one?"

"I do," I responded as I looked at all the armed men around me, showing by my expression that perhaps there was some hope in opening a dialogue. "I am divorced, and I have one child."

"You still have your child," he said.

"Yes," I said. "He lives with his mother."

"Have you ever thought of what it would be like to lose your son? Have you ever asked yourself what you would do if your son lost his life?"

"Yes, I have. I think every mother and father thinks about it. It would definitely be the worst-possible moment in any parent's life."

"Well, Detective, I have done more than just think about it. I have lived it! It happened to me, and it was not my mistake or my wife's mistake or my daughter's mistake. Nevertheless, my daughter is dead, and she only lived to be ten years old! The people responsible for her death went on with their lives as if nothing had happened. They were never held accountable, never forced to face the consequences. They were responsible for her death, but they were never punished."

"So you decided to kill them, just to get revenge," I said. "And why did you decide to kill them in the way that you did?"

"That was the only fun part of it," he said. "To find a theme in the killing, and what better way to do it than in the way we feed, slaughter and prepare ducks in southwestern France!"

"I would not have thought a man like you would do

something so sick and disturbed," I told him, keeping my voice calm and even in tone. "I thought you had more class and honor than that."

"It was actually just a suggestion on my part. The Handler played the role to perfection though, I must admit."

I looked at Michel. The Handler was either a nickname Dumont had given the hit man or one the man had chosen for himself. We'd seen no reference to the name in the killer's copious notes.

"Mr. Dumont, what are you looking for now, and how do you envision the outcome of all this?" I asked, adding, "Time is not on your side."

"I am almost done with my wine, Detective," he said. "Just two more sips. Tell me, what can I expect to encounter in jail in the US?"

"As mastermind of three connected murders in three different states, which also resulted in the murder of a fourth innocent victim, we will take you to a federal penitentiary, where you will spend the rest of your life."

"Not really exciting, if I may say so," he responded. "I am sure American prison food is pretty much the same as French, and the conditions of imprisonment the same as here."

"Not a bright future at all," I said. I knew I was taking a risk by keeping him talking. I had a pretty good idea how this story was going to end.

"Detective," he said, "I will open the electronic door now. I am ready, and I feel pretty good. Perfect timing, I should say. Thank you for listening to me and allowing me to finish my wine."

At that, I felt the tension build in the room, with all the weapons pointed at the heavy wooden door.

There was a sudden click, followed by a long loud beep, and then, finally, the door opened slightly.

"Charles Dumont, put your weapon down, and come

out with your hands on your head!" Michel commanded.

After a few seconds of silence, we heard the mastermind say, "I love you, Jocelyn; here I come, Emilia. ..."

There was a split second of silence, and then a shotgun blast rang through the underground chamber.

I knew it was going to end up this way.

The RAID team stormed the inner room, only to find our man on the floor, with half his head gone and a beautiful shotgun in his right hand.

After the lieutenant said the room was clear, Michel and I entered. Inside this beautiful cellar were a marble table and two wrought-iron chairs. A bottle of Romanée-Conti La Tâche was on the table—1992, the year of his daughter's birth. An empty glass was next to the bottle, with a short note beside it.

I approached the table and read the note: "I would rather save the taxpayers money for the next forty years. I have hurt enough people already. I am sorry for that, but I am happy to rejoin my Emilia."

With a tired face, I looked at Michel. "Case closed," I said.

Chapter 60

I sat in a sophisticated wine bar at Charles de Gaulle Airport, waiting for my flight back to the states.

My cell phone rang, and I took it out of my pocket. "Detective Sebastien Saint-Gemmes," I said, looking at the vast array of wines on the menu.

"Hey, Seb. It's Moose. Did I catch you at a bad time?"

"No. Actually, I am just relaxing, trying to decide between an Anjou red and a Chinon to go with my appetizer."

"Tough choice," he replied with a smile in his voice. "I'm just calling to make sure you're scheduled to depart on time so I'll know when to pick you up at the airport here in Omaha like we planned."

"Yes, so far so good; no late departure to Minneapolis, and the weather seems fine, so I should land on time."

"All right. Call or text me if anything changes."

"I will," I replied. "Thank you for checking on me, brother."

Moose laughed.

As I always said, he was the best friend a man could have.

After putting my phone away, I decided to go with a fresh glass of Cabernet Franc from Anjou in the Loire Valley. This wine was going to be perfect with the simple appetizer of sautéed veal sweetbreads, served with a Dijon mustard sauce and a bed of fresh lettuce. I placed my order with a charming young waitress, and then I started to admire the newly remodeled Terminal F.

I soon caught myself thinking about Erica. The last few

days had been crazy, between the shoot-out in Paris and the suicide of Charles Dumont in Madiran, and I realized that I had not even had the chance to talk to her directly. I had called FBI Special Agent Gary Duval from the private plane on the way back to Paris from Madiran, as I was responsible for letting him know how the case had wrapped up. Duval had told me that a team was getting ready to bring the assassin's body back to the US, with the help of the embassy. He also wanted to thank Michel for the help we had received from Interpol and the local authorities. The job was done without too much of an outcry or bad publicity from anybody in France. The US media, on the other hand, was all over the fact that the case had been closed and justice had been served in honor of the three chefs killed.

My food arrived, and I shifted my focus from the case to the lovely meal in front of me. The appetizer was perfect. The sweetbreads were cooked to perfection, with a creamy texture that merged perfectly with the pungency of the strong mustard and the delicate fresh lettuce. A freshly baked baguette was served on the side, most welcome at the end of the meal to sauce the bottom of the plate. I knew doing that was not really proper in some countries, but for me, it was a sign that the person had really enjoyed the food to the last drop. I knew firsthand that the chef would not be upset to see my dish come back completely clean.

"Embarquement dans quinze minutes en destination de Minneapolis, Porte 5," a soft female voice announced over the PA system.

Perfect! I had fifteen minutes before boarding my flight; just enough time for a nice espresso to complete my meal.

After paying my bill, I called Erica's number, even though it was pretty early in Las Vegas. I just wanted to hear her voice and tell her I missed her.

"Hello, Sebastien," she said in a sleepy, sexy voice.

"Good morning to you, Miss Erica," I said. "I am sorry to

257

wake you up early like this, but I wanted to hear your voice before boarding the plane."

"No worries, Seb. It's actually time for me to wake up, and I am glad to hear your voice instead of the alarm. How are you doing? Are you bringing me any souvenirs from Paris?"

"I did not really have time for shopping."

"I know; I'm teasing you. Gary called to keep me in the loop as things progressed in France. I am glad you made it without any problems. Your cousin okay?"

"Oh yes, he is a tough Italian bird. But thank you for asking." I paused and then added, "Listen, Erica, I was wondering if I could see you again … hopefully, not in a professional way but on a more private level."

There was a brief silence on the other end of the line that seemed to last for centuries.

"Are you asking me out, Sebastien?"

"Yes, I am. I know it would be a long-distance relationship, but we could try it if you are up for it."

"I would love to."

"I have to board the plane now, but I will call you as soon as I arrive in Omaha."

"I can't wait, Seb," she said before hanging up the phone.

I stayed at the bar for an extra minute, soon realizing that I was sweating and my heart was racing. Was I falling in love?

Epilogue

The weekend after I returned from France I was back working the line in the Drunken Frog, filling the orders as they came off the printer. It was nice to be wielding my chef's knife again, and I tried to put behind me the gruesome case my cousin and I had just closed in France. That had been one of the most convoluted cases of my career, and I hoped no future case would be grislier.

My recent trip had inspired tonight's special, and I sighed as I plated the cassoulet. I would always grieve the loss of my friends, and I would always miss them, but life had to go on. I had a lot to look forward to with Erica, and I really wanted our relationship to work. I figured a long-distance romance would not be too difficult for me; after all, I already juggled being a full-time homicide detective *and* a chef/restaurateur. How hard could it be to live in Omaha when my girlfriend lived in Vegas? I was falling in love, so everything seemed doable and possible. ...

Just as I was smiling at all the possibilities, I felt my phone vibrate in my pocket. I stopped to check it, in case it was the office.

"Yes, Boss?" I said when Randy Lewis's number came up on my screen.

"We've got a homicide, Saint-Gemmes. So much for your night off."

"On it, Boss," I said, as I listened to his instructions and walked out of the kitchen to let Moose know someone would have to cover for me for the rest of the night.

My heart would always be in the kitchen, but as a detective, the street and the safety of the citizens of Omaha always had to come first.

About the Author

Cedric Fichepain was born in 1972. He grew up in France and Italy, and he and his wife, Desarae, moved to the United States in 1997.They live in Omaha, Nebraska, with their three sons.

Cedric is a certified executive chef (CEC). He is the owner and chef of Le Voltaire French Restaurant and Le Petit Paris French Bakery, both in Omaha. In addition, Cedric is a part-time instructor at the Institute for the Culinary Arts, and a member of the Hall of Fame of the Omaha Restaurant Association. He and his co-writer, Barbee Davis, published and produced the play *20 Percent and Counting,* a work that chronicles the tribulations of the daily life of a waiter.

Cedric's passion for fine food began at a young age, as he was always surrounded by his mother's and grandmothers' cooking. One day he decided to mix his lifelong love of cooking with his love of crime fiction, and his first book, *Fowl to the Bone,* was born.